SAINTS + SINNERS

2024
NEW POETRY
FROM THE FESTIVAL

SAINTS + SINNERS

2024
NEW POETRY
FROM THE FESTIVAL

With an Introduction by our judge
Chen Chen

Edited by
Jan Edwards Hemming & Paul J. Willis

Saints+Sinners
2024

Published in the United States of America by
REBEL SATORI PRESS
rebelsatori.com

SAINTS + SINNERS
2024 NEW POETRY FROM THE FESTIVAL

ISBN: 978-1-60864-301-1

Credits
Editors: Jan Edwards Hemming and Paul J. Willis
Cover Photo by Jacob Mitchell
Cover Design by Toan Nguyen
Book Design by Sven Davisson

Contents

* Winner, 2024 Saints and Sinners Poetry Contest
** Runner-Up, 2024 Saints and Sinners Poetry Contest

ACKNOWLEDGMENTS

We would like to thank:

The John Burton Harter Foundation for their continued generous support of the Saints and Sinners Literary Festival.

Susanne Scovern, Scovern Law Firm, for generously underwriting our poetry contests.

Jacob Mitchell, cover artist for the 2024 Saints and Sinners poetry anthology.

Everyone who has entered the contest and/or attended the Saints and Sinners Literary Festival over the last twenty-one years for their energy, ideas, and dedication in keeping the written LGBTQ word alive.

Previous Winners

2023
Isobel A. Burke

2022
Michael Montlack

2021
Danielle Bero

Judge's Introduction

Sinful is the level of my delight in presenting this gathering of divinities a.k.a. poems. This bouquet of marvels. Poetry by LGBTQ+ writers is not-so-secretly my favorite kind of poetry to read. Why read about cishet people looking at flowers when you can read about LGBTQ+ people wearing flowers…or altogether reimagining them, each stem and petal, reconfiguring the very concept of the floral into a portal—elsewhere?

I have been known to employ hyperbole (stating things dramatically? me??), but it's no exaggeration to say I was filled with the giddiest gratitude to get to serve as judge for the 2024 Saints and Sinners Poetry Contest. I was eager to submit to each of the eighteen finalists' submissions, their messy and magnificent transformations. What a theme: "transformation." What an honor: to be so altered by these words.

Invention may very well be another name for an LGBTQ+ life. Reinvention is every LGBTQ+ person's secret (or not-so-secret) middle name. I find myself returning to these blazing, defiant sentences of Ocean Vuong's: "Being queer saved my life. Often we see queerness as deprivation. But when I look at my life, I saw that queerness demanded an alternative innovation from me. I had to make alternative routes; it made me curious; it made me ask, 'Is this enough for me?'"

Each poet in this anthology has looked again and again at their life and transformed that looking into true reckoning, transformed life into a new aliveness. No word is taken for granted; no breath is left unexamined or unexploded. I am so moved by how these poets remake language and a whole range of subjects—from family and mortality to sex and snow, from crows and school to mint and legend and the multilingual and the extraterrestrial and more. More.

Of course, it was difficult to choose a winner and two runners-up from such astonishing entries. A different judge would choose differently. But for me, the following three poets went beyond the transformative to reach…I don't know. And when reading for contests, I'm always seeking that "I don't know." I'm seeking—how else to put it—those poems that refuse to give up seeking, refuse to turn away from their deeply vulnerable and idiosyncratic questions. Poems that ultimately, entirely evade my descriptive powers. But I'll try—and thankfully, I can quote from these poets' powerful work.

In "Virga," Wayne Johns offers an elegy that cuts through a sea of platitudes, silences, and cruelties—finding not answers but a kind of sacred mystery, deeper waters. In other (better) words: "First recorded // decades ago, many have searched but no one's ever found / the whale. Only its call."

In "What is it tends you?" Ben Kline manages to weave together equal parts anxiety and tenderness in lines so piercing in their insight, unforgettable in their imagery. For example: "Dad says he keeps busy looking // for ways to stay busy, to ignore time / doing what time does: gray hair, / the lily's white hood curling // into a brown coffin after the pollen / salts the pot soil."

And in "August," Holly Zhou, the winner of the 2024 Saints and Sinners Poetry Contest, deftly shifts from comedy ("a cockroach falls over my dinner. / In my shock, I forget how to say the word / in Chinese, & for a few minutes / we scream *BIG BUG!*") to something like tragedy ("How wrong is it / to feel happy, if my solidarity / is selfish?") and back again, before arriving at a new place, a beautifully weird tone and a not-quite-home, a field not-empty, an ever-learning self within ever-shifting community. As the speaker says, "I have more than my shoulders to lean on" and "if I look a meter to the left, / listen harder— / a tree, perhaps, or the sound / of crickets singing."

I applaud the poets of this deceptively slim and actually vast anthology. I want to keep hanging out in their poems; let me linger in the strange and luminous and insect-filled corners. I am all the queerer and bolder, knowing I am writing alongside these interrupters of the usual, these dreamers of the incendiary and not so impossible.

Chen Chen
Judge, 2024 Saints and Sinners Poetry Contest

Editor's Note

During the early summer months of my childhood, I plucked cicada husks from trees and collected them in a Mason jar. I once peeled open a cocoon, desperate to understand the process happening beneath the silky white threads. The Byrds' song "Turn! Turn! Turn! (To Everything There Is a Season)" brought inexplicable tears to my seven-year-old eyes, as I listened and rewound, listened and rewound. I was (and remain) entranced by the magic of fairy tales and fantasy: straw turns into bricks of gold, a mermaid becomes a girl, a white horse is raised from the dead. In short, transformations have long been at both the literal and figurative core of the things that engage my imagination most powerfully.

And yet, I've struggled to embrace my own metamorphoses through the years. No matter how big or small the transformation may be, from clothing size to relationship status, change so often feels to me like an admission of not being good enough. If someone—especially my mother—can see said change in my life, does that not mean I have failed in some way? Even positive shifts can seem like revelations of my shortcomings, my losses, my inability to get things right the first time.

Perhaps that is why I found myself so immersed in these poems. Of course, on the line- and image-levels, the eighteen finalists' work is exquisitely wrought, but my reading experience felt more personal than that. As I experienced Nat Gove's rendering of disordered eating, Acie Clark's delicious Southern dirge, Wayne Johns' treatment of the passage of time, Agnes Hanying Ong's mystification of common phrases, and Nayelly Barrios' visceral interpretations of thirst, I was *there*; I was *them*.

In this collection of poems, I found, at long last, companions on my journey of struggling with finding self-acceptance, coming out, moving cities, changing careers, ending and beginning and rediscovering identities and relationships of all kinds. In reflecting (pun intended), I couldn't help but picture *The Neverending Story*'s Mirrorgate at the Southern Oracle: these poems showed me who I am and, more importantly, reminded me that I am not alone as I navigate life's inevitable iterations and my own feelings surrounding them.

It is my second year compiling the Saints and Sinners Poetry Contest Anthology, and I have yet again been resoundingly reminded of the power of queer poetry. To echo judge Chen Chen's sentiment, these poems not only explore transformations but also offer a transformative experience for their readers. I have tried to lay out the poems in a way that embraces all of the ups and downs and turn-arounds, the yeses and nos and maybes, the bitter laughter and lush tears—and, most of all, the *possibilities*—of the journey that is being LGBTQ+.

I hope that these poems take you on the same magical mystery tour of language, love, loss, longing, and legitimizing on which they compelled me.

Jan Edwards Hemming
Editor, 2024 Saints and Sinners Poetry Contest

Holly Zhou

Winner, 2024 Saints and Sinners Poetry Contest

August

i.
I've been searching for another
entry point, some pronoun
outside "I."

The parties down the block
blast versions of devotion:
I want this, I want that.

Speed it up, I pray. *Savor me
all at once.* But they can't hear me,
my new roommates—
my mosquitoes, my spiders, my ants.

My skins swell, drunk
beneath my nails.

ii.
During their comedy set, Sabrina Wu reenacts
one of their coming out conversations.
You think I like this body?
their father replied. *You think I want this
face, this skin, these eyes?*

My eyes fill & suddenly the air
feels heavy, refuses to move through me.
I can't stop the tears & the photographer

1

won't stop pointing at me like I'm the star
student. I wipe my face with wet hands,
cover my eyes. *Don't look at me,* I want
to protest. *I'm not laughing.*

iii.
I've moved, I say, finally breaking
my father the news, *to another
state.* Halfway through the long
distance static, *What's
your address?* I scream
because a cockroach falls over my dinner.
In my shock, I forget how to say the word
in Chinese, & for a few minutes
we scream *BIG BUG!*
蟑螂
What?!
蟑螂 *? !* back & forth until the animal
finds shelter in the furnace. *Those aren't too bad,*
he says. I don't bother divulging the details—
that the Southern species has evolved
flight, that their legs materialize on mine
without warning. *You get any rats yet?* & lists what
pellets & powders I should purchase, on top of
the replacement window screens for the mosquitoes,
the traps, the sprays, how all this is because I refused
to spend more for a nice apartment, makes me
promise that I'll return to a job that pays. I give up
on searching, decide to leave the insect alone.

iv.
Because we're in Brooklyn, & because
Sabrina headlined, the audience is entirely one
or both of queer & Asian.
After the show, people buzz
with the promise

2

of unmade plans. I flit at the edges,
unsure. I find someone new
& I find someone I haven't spoken to
in years. Less than a month left here.

Any of my Thursdays turned
sacred by scarcity. We hitch a ride
across the Manhattan Bridge, mouth along
to choruses we'd never admit to loving, sprint
into H-Mart seconds before closing.
Just one makgeolli, we plead.

We toast to time, bum bits
of our lives off one another.
Summers in Taiwan, art school,
how we're each the eldest sibling.

v.
My parents used to tell me to be
a good sister, to behave & lead
by example.

Gratitude & relief when neither
of my siblings turns out to be
straight. How wrong is it
to feel happy, if my solidarity
is selfish?

vi.
Before I left Brooklyn, my partner sent me a set
of poems. In it, she wrote, *You / are the poet /
The falling apart is different every
day.* I'm convinced that I'm the *you* & I'm not
convinced about the poet.

I reopen the scabs on my arms. There's too much

3

I want to hold. The lines cross over.

I'm still learning.

That the field outside isn't
empty, that I have more than
my shoulders to lean on.

That if I look a meter to the left,
listen harder—
a tree, perhaps, or the sound
of crickets singing.

For Jenny Who Shares My Birthday

The day we found out, we knew we could trust
nothing & no one. Time mirrored itself, a simple
sleight of hand. Your face for mine. The second

time we met, waiting in the same line at the same
sold-out live show in Manhattan—*you* listen
to him, *too?*—I was already suspicious.

The third time I saw my face, it was a different
island. *How* did we end up in the *same*
seat in the *same* restaurant with the *same*
bride in *Honolulu?* we screamed

in all caps. I reassured you that I didn't believe
in silly stars, but I requested yours
just in case. The truth revealed, we knew

we must wake as each other's
cockroach. The same compound
eyes & crooked legs. Contorted spines.

On our fated anniversary, I leave, an unexcused
absence from my office desk & my twenty-seventh
hour-long expectations planning sync for this
quarter, which is about to end. I don't care.

You don't either. You call me, your voice
ringing like an arcade jackpot—did you know
we can get hotpot today, for *free?*—& so I scurry

to sit across from you, one leg looping
a cup of ice water, another lugging
a hot water, & you gape at me, appalled,

as I start ordering twenty-seven
dishes. Of course we can finish it! Besides,
it's *free*! It's all you can eat! Each time you brandish
your jaws, the pieces glide into my gizzard—
halves of lotus root, halves of taro, halves of
dumplings, halves of halves of corn—until three
hours later, we are still feasting, the wealthiest

of emperors, & the possibilities begin
to protrude from our stomachs. If we can eat
like *this*, then why can't we *also* quit

our jobs? We're young! Move to Berlin!
We tip the establishment, strut out the doors,
swinging. Our faces are shining, & all around us,
people are entering & exiting the subways as if

nothing's happening, & we cannot fathom
a tomorrow when that will be us, because today
we have eaten the afternoon & we still have more

growth to achieve—a dozen donuts, a fruit
smoothie, a coffee—all free, & we can ride the train
to Brooklyn, inkstain our shelled skins, because we can

pay three-quarters the price, & these things
won't be up tomorrow. Not for us.

For obvious reasons, we must die
at the same time. We will know when

to close our eyes, & I will wave my antennae
toward yours. I will broadcast

visions, pheromones, wireless transmissions—
banquets, rolls of kimbap, endless donuts &

discounts—as we row from this life to the next,
as we float our bodies in the warmest of waters.

Runoff

I watched my life trickle down
in the car wash runoff. Felt it
collect dirt, lick across
the driveway, plunge quickly
toward my toes.

I veered away from the sound.
Slunk deeper into the castle.

Soaked my hair, braided it, wound it
until it smiled. Every day, I woke to
the gilded dream: white teeth,
gold ring, white marble staircase.

The first rule of dreams: labeling a body
an angel does not grant it wings.

I shone brightly, orbited
the moat, my steps light,
my strides fluent.

I spent the years sleepwalking.
What I learned best, I could do
with eyes closed—
effortlessness, a two-handed
gesture, beauty.

The second rule: labeling a body an angel
does not grant it eyes.

They adjusted slowly—a bird's-
eye view of itself. The sky slid
like satin, fizzled static. Through the lace—

its limp gaze, the gully, the body grayed
with liquid. Slipping.

It took many dreams before I could look
back. Before I knew what was necessary.
I swapped out my arms.
Flew of my own accord.

Left the bedside prayers, the water
to the corpse, the window to the prince.

Labeling a body an angel does not grant it
a body. There exists no magic kiss.

No slipper carved from glass. I wished for
a knife, a chisel, anything to break
the perfect fit. There must be some
shape or shadow, some dark

marrow beyond the moat, a cup
that can bear all these layers
of desire.

I bite my tongue, step out
of my fists. Crumple my skin
into the murky waters.

The Daughter and the Crow

after Richard Siken

1

This is a story about a woman. A man sees the woman, marries her, builds a house at the edge of the forest, and the two live happily. Until his mother flies over the ocean, opens the door, the drawers, the windows, *Where is the baby? I brought you clothes for the son*, and the woman grows full with shame, says, *Thank you.* Begins praying.

One night, the woman dreams of needles piercing her back, metal cold against her belly, gloved hands prying apart her skin and pulling out a body. The man wakes from the woman's screams. *I dreamt I was pregnant.* The man turns back on his side. *About time*, he says.

No, she insists. *The baby was wet. Covered in black feathers. His nose was black. Small and curved downward.*

Like a beak? he asks. *A crow? No*, she says. *It means I'll die giving birth.* The man tells the woman not to be stupid. *Crows are good luck. They find precious things. This means our son won't be like other sons. He'll take care of us when we're old. Bring us meat and riches.*

2

This is a story about a woman and a man. Every night after, the woman feels the hands, the metal, screams until the crows take pity and grant the pair a daughter. The woman understands now what the feathers meant.

10

The daughter is born healthy. Learns quickly how to find things. Names them: leaf, tree, green, black, bark, bird. When she carries enough words, the mother teaches her a lesson. *This is what it means to have a daughter*, she tells her child. *One day you must give your daughter away. But sons, that's a different story. Sons stay in the family.* The daughter cries. *But I don't want to be sold. I want to stay.*

Don't be silly, the mother says. *You'll understand when you're older. A man will find you and he will give you his name and you will fly away. Pray that you'll have a son.*

3

This is a story about a daughter. The daughter leaves for her first day of school. During lunch, the children play House. Her friends pretend to get married, and the daughter plays their daughter. She bakes bread in the pretend oven, sets the table with the pretend silverware, and serves a feast to her pretend parents in their pretend castle.

Now it's time for you to pretend to run away, her pretend parents say. The daughter is a fast learner, is good at this game. She runs to the copse at the edge of the playground and climbs onto the low branches of a tree. When she stands on her toes, she can see the roof of her home. She can see through the kitchen windows, through the parted blinds to her parents at the table, sipping tea and preparing lunch in silence.

Overhead, the leaves rustle as a bird lands, adjusts its footing. *Caw, caw.*

The daughter looks up. The bird watches the daughter wait.

Before the bell rings, her friend, the pretend neighbor, runs to find her in the forest. Calls out her name.

4

This is a story about a daughter and a mother. *We played House at school today*, she tells her mother. *No wonder. Don't run around outside so much. Your skin already looks darker. Cover yourself.*

The daughter hides her arms behind her back. Continues, *What if I marry a princess? Would that mean I'm the prince?* The mother blinks. *I suppose it would*, she replies.

So I'd be a son?

Don't be stupid. Don't waste your time with these games. No one will want you if you keep acting like this.

5

This is a story about a daughter who pretends to be a daughter. The children play House again and the daughter pretends to run away again, this time together with her pretend neighbor. They enter a clearing and sit on a tree stump. Face each other so that the dirt on their shoes barely touch. The daughter reaches down, picks up a handful of dried leaves, layers them across her arms. The daughter asks her friend, *What if we marry?*

Each other?
Yeah.
That's gross. You're not a boy.
I meant pretend *marry. I can* pretend *to be a rich prince.*
Okay, then.
Okay. So should we kiss?

The friend no longer wants to be her friend. The girl runs back to the pretend castle, tells the pretend daughter not to come back.

6

This a story about a daughter who no one wanted to be a daughter.

The daughter steps onto a branch, strips off its leaves as she climbs up, sticks them onto her arm. The sap trickles over her skin like white veins. She rubs the sap over her legs, her ankles, her belly. Rubs her hands, sticky and white, over her eyes.

The school bell rings. Her pretend friend and her pretend parents don't call her name. The bird cleans its feathers.

The daughter climbs higher, higher than the children in the classrooms and higher than her parents in the kitchen, filling her fists with green and green. She wonders what it must feel like, to be as light as the wind. To go anywhere, touch anything, sound beautiful.

The mother takes a sip. The daughter lifts her arms. The bird takes flight.

Jeremy Graves

The Grand Entrance of the Drag Queen Jenna Gravy

1. Most Wanted Poem

The offensive idea of beauty has persisted more in poems than
    in any other art.
Hi, my name's Jenna, and I like to dance in a non-alliterative
    dress.
My dress is so ugly, but not so ugly in a beautiful way.

I jerk off to the absent beauty of my poems. When I shoot, I
    shout the name
Of a wealthy collector who finances my work but would feel
    embarrassed to be mentioned in this particular context.
I interrogate my poems under pain of the beautiful poem.

;-)

Hi, it's me again: Jenna. I know you're there. Please pick up
    your animatronic face.
I want you to know I started going to group again, this time
    with flies.
I spread honey on my face. Inside my dress. You know the one.

It lay dormant for the longest time in storage.
I only rediscovered it as the flood threatened moist endeavor.
So, I piled all my dresses in the front yard, high on a hill, as a
    prophylactic.
But of course, the minute I put them out, collectors flocked to
    my house.

14

They must have seen the kaleidoscope from Google Earth.

They swooped in, masturbating furiously to the blunt display of
    soaked dresses
That, sadly, can never form a poem, due to their chirality.

;-)

Stop it, just stop it. Not here. Not on the page. With children
    next door to the page.

When I sold my last poem for a million dollars,[1] at first I felt
    smug,
Like I'd sold some gold-plated shit, but then I remembered the
    incorruptibility of poems, how no page can hold them,
And then I felt guilty, realizing that, in the long run, the gold
    would peel away, to reveal
—*Oh, gasp! Victorian swoon and verlkemptness!*—
To reveal my shitty face.

So, as you strip off my dress, consider this: do you seek to
    remove unloveliness
From your orbit, or to reveal the panoply of my chest?

;-)

I'm tired of Manhattan. I want to go somewhere, like, really,
    truly obscene
But upscale, like a ring of Saturn, or the Marianas Trench
For a poet's retreat. To collect natural specimens for poems.
But in no way do we assemble beauty from the rejects of the
    sea.

---

1 Future editors of my work, adjust this number upward to keep pace with
inflation. Convert "dollars" into whatever currency is most glamorous in your
time.

And if—*big* if—we're doing Moby Dick role-play, then you
know what to call me. Call me Jenna.

2. Jenna and You Go Cruising

Mmmmmmm. A poem. And the musk of a poem.

Aaahhhhhhhh. A whip. And the tautologies of a whip.

You're a bad little reader, aren't you?, handcuffed to the page.
But my wordplay can redeem you in an instant,
Because the Divine intersects the flow of time at a right angle,
    like sunlight on the water's surface,
Which sets the whole ecology of Grindr in motion,

Pulverizing us into glitter.

;-)

I'd like to sing a barcarolle for this next set
As the poem floats like a coffin
Down the Grand Canal of Venice, CA.

(Bend over, Harry Styles. We're passing under the Bridge of
    Sighs.)

Ah, my vaping closets us in mist!
Ah, you're a gentleman, Harry, and I'm whatever insect
    pollinates a gentleman!

Honey-
suckle, you can't move, stuck here on my gondola, but I can fly
Through these lines, my fog machine of words
Lending atmosphere. Right, Harry? Right?!

Noooootiiiiice meeeee, Angel of Glamour!

16

;-)

In this grungy dungeon glory
Hole of a bathroom, they say Kafka
First conceived of his masterpiece, *The Metamorphosis*.

Scrawled on the wall: "Call Cockroach for a good time."

So I do it. I dial the number that summons
The Man Who Would Be Cockroach.

Rumors scuttle between stalls.
The phone rings for decades.

Finally, as I reach the end of my unnatural life,
An inhuman voice whispers, "Hello?"

;-)

Don't ask who dreamed these lines. Don't ask who reads them.
It's better that we love each other in the dark.

If you really knew me, you'd find me too beautiful for words
    like these.
And if I really knew you, I'd shrug under the weight of your
    gaze,
Heavy with centuries of books and their classical need for
    honesty.

Reader, let me be that badass bitch who infests your mind with
    freedom
From dignity. Ride with me long enough, and you'll forget
The heartache of Dickinson, the slow stubble burn and mystic
    American cock of Whitman.
Let me be your laughing gas, on tap. I'll fill you up.

Promise me, hunty, you won't sashay away. At least, not tonight.

3. Astrophil as Jenna

Pinned down the other night in a ditch,
The wind rummaging through my skirt,
I looked up at Betelgeuse and could almost remember
How, before the Big Bang, that star and I
And every corner of the universe were touching.
(I felt sorry for Betelgeuse, burning for me from so far away.)

It's a drag to be so beautiful no one knows you're human.
To go through life as the ghost of Marilyn Monroe.
To get tackled by the wind because your curves threaten
Nature itself. Maybe that's why, when the sun rose
Like a wound over the planet, no sorry anonymous
Father figure carried me to the nearest hospital.

I'd prefer to ascend into the Milky Way.
There, Warhol would take me by the hand and say,
"Condragulations, you've finally arrived."
Mesmerized, he'd paint me over and over
Until the stars go out, and only I remain
Standing—since a girl this stunning ain't born to die.

4. Jenna Untucked

I'm beautiful because I say I'm beautiful.

Look at me. I injected stomach fat into my ass,
Forming the-ass-that-launched-a-thousand-ships.
Look at me, asshole. I'm going to change the world
By walking all over it in flaming stilettos.

You call me insincere. Like, when I flirt with Presidents,
My worldwide charm is only silicon-deep.

18

But honestly, do you think I've never stared down a mirror
At my washed face, so desolate as to seem featureless,
And that the horror of my own unloveliness
Didn't descend upon me like an iron cage

So that I lifted my shaking hand, picked up the most
Ridiculous makeup I could find, and painted on
A new way of being, in a red so vibrant it could be blood?

5. Jenna Works the Strip

I gallop in, dress hoisted up my legs like a red flag, astride the
    shoulders of a slobbering beefcake!
Because I'm a Poet. Meaning I auction off every angle of my
    body.
Every line, every lacuna.

Go on. Try my gorgeous, sesquipedalian tuna.

Because you haven't lived if you don't read the next line I write.

;-)

Tragedy: *Nel mezzo del cammin di nostra vita,*
I discover every cliché ever born
Has attached itself by delicate, almost invisible strings
To the art I have chosen.

They follow me around like a train of cans tinkling on the
    ground,
For I am the Queen of Meat.

What do I do about it, you ask?
I smile like a bitch in heat.

I own my clichés.

Because a man in rouge can outfox a woman on a bad day.
Because a man in rouge dies over and over.

Because a man.

;-)

It hurts: tender little nibbles along my penumbra
Accomplished by a wealthy patron who only tells me his
    nickname
But never the secret, eternal name that frees his wallet.

"Buy all my poems," I blurt out in a moment of weakness,
Forgetting this is business:
"Oh, all of them, even the ones that aren't about me!"

;-)

With the sadness of green roses tossed upon a stage,
Under a raging light bulb that bubbles and hisses incandescent
    terror,
In a haze less glamorous than red,
I wobble on the pole. I threaten to stumble.

High rollers hold their breath.
The world economy hiccups…

But then I death drop into the splits, and it's so freaking obvious
All of it was intentional: the wobble, the paraphernalia, the
    despair,

My coy disregard for gravity.

Nat Gove

Everything Goes Back on the Shelf

In order to lose a few pounds
I stretch my legs up,
pedal an imaginary bike
through the air after every meal
while I think about what I ate
the day before, and the day before that.
I have an eating disorder.
If I had more sex I could
burn one hundred calories
each time; at least
that is what my German friend told me.
She missed having sex
with her boyfriend,
felt like her body showed it;
she borrowed bananas
from her host mom's kitchen
as a substitution. I count
the number of groceries
in the shopping cart:
the total has to equal a product of five.
My head will spin,
not like an owl's.
Everything goes back on the shelf
if the number is not right,
even the Riesen Chocolate Chews
I earned by doing thirty minutes
of pedaling,
two rounds of sex
last week with my partner.

Sex with myself does not count;
it is forbidden.
That was what my church said
about masturbation:
it is lustful,
an act of sin
against the body,
the temple of the holy spirit,
where an ape sits on a throne
eating a banana
from my German friend's vagina.

Dear Mother,

I molded my body to fit into your frame,
so skinny I could be hung on a hanger
in a recovery center with other women
eating their hair for nutrients
and drinking the wind to keep down
the calorie count.

Your mother stood confused at the mirror,
wondered who the old silver-haired figure
was looking back, pinching her hips,
telling us both in the room
she was too wide to fit into the jeans
she wore yesterday.

I smelled the meatloaf
baking in the oven, onions
and bread crumbs crispy.
You cut thick slices for me
and I watched you stare
at your serving until it turned
into a lettuce leaf,
sprouting out from the plate
covered in dew.

Your brother took his thumb
and index finger,
pinched the skin underneath
my belly button and said,
"Hold off on the donuts."

I bought another dozen
and swallowed them whole
until the glaze turned my tongue

to crystal. I sliced into
his abdomen with my anger.

You turned into a whisper;
I cannot find your shadow,
only my own silhouette,
waiting to be traced
by a dressmaker, turned
into a pattern of curves and movement.
My shape is a plate full of carbohydrates
marching onto my palette
as your early summer cabbage
patch waits to be harvested.

audibly sighing from my own denied disorder in the checkout line

Possibly from avoidance;
admitting to being unaware of my fingers,
or if I am actually okay with the thickness
of my freshly sliced deli meat
handed to me from the man behind the counter,
remembering only the moment
I grabbed the knife yesterday,
the one with grape jelly
on one side of the blade,
on account of its sharp edge
because I like the feeling
of scraping against my skin,
and even today,
while staring at the cover of *People* magazine,
skinny airbrushed legs and anti-frizz hair,
my mind is living in the past:
the first time I made myself throw up a Wendy's frosty,
and only acidic milky froth came out, I still
acknowledge what I disown about my shape,
even if not with my heart pumping,
counting items in my grocery cart,
parasympathetic nervous system yelling,
Did you count the bag of apples individually
or the whole bag as one item? flash of familiarity
of things I despise about myself,
the way my fingers turn purple
when I grab for a box of waffles from the freezer,
with the obligation to speak to myself so detestable,
Could you have brushed your rat's nest hair
before going out in public? impulsivity always grabs me
when I have no desire to dig deeper
to find meaning, *What is that late 90s soft rock song*

playing right now in the store?
one that I fear will crack open my skull
to reveal a deeper story or identification,
Oh, never mind, I know this song, it's Backstreet Boys.
I am constantly explaining, excusing myself
for behaviors I tire of having no control over,
like curling up on the floor
between the scent of fresh bouquets
and hot bar macaroni and cheese,
but then the control might be
the mechanism I utilize for safety,
I hope I have enough on my SNAP card.
I have many dust bunnies
needing vacuuming
by a prescription from the pharmacy
at the back of the store
where the line wraps around a display of pistachios,
I am sensitive
to doses higher than ten milligrams
and allergic to walnuts; my lips swell
and my tongue breaks out into a map of red welts
called Geographic Tongue. Without whimpering
about the passing of years where pain
built itself into a grave or the amount of time
I have been standing in this line,
digging for myself,
as a private survivor of my own misery, a hole
into the middle of this bag of chewy blueberry bagels,
where I hunt for a demon
or the leprechaun from the Lucky Charms box
I put back on the shelf twice,
I tell myself, *I'm fine.*

There are fragmentary truths out of my great sadness
in which everything whole has been hammered
into small particles of happiness residue,

26

which feels sticky like the handle of this shopping cart
where some toddler has taken initiative
to taint this public food transporting device
with mystery goo, yes, just as not to see
the nothingness of my situation,
everything is ripe and ready
like the satsumas were last autumn
on the tree I forgot to prune,
like decisions that I have not committed to,
waiting to be picked out
of my grocery cart and stuffed
into a plastic bag.

Acie Clark

Small Talk

Thursday
The coffee was good. The morning is young.
I am making eye contact with the red dog
while he shits under a pink magnolia tree.
People on the internet inform me that this
(the shitting with the sustained eye contact)
is a demonstration of trust, is vulnerability
in its most practical iteration.
Will you come watch me write this poem?
Can I bear to let you see me change?
Pink blooms around the red dog.
February is March in Alabama.
I am trying to remember
I have something to say.

Friday
The coffee was good. The morning was slow.
The first known use of "morning" in English
was the 13th century. My students ask how old
this language is. It depends on who you ask.
In the scheme of things, so young, having only
existed for some sum of hundreds of years.
My students think I am kind of old; I realize,
in the scheme of things, I am so young, having
only existed for some twenty-six years.
I am too old to not know how very young I am.
Everyone else can see me being young,
like the woman stopping to fix her skirt
in the window of that Suzanne Vega song.

Imagine me fixing my tie in the window of this poem,
on my way to convince my students that anything,
let alone Chaucer, still matters. I understand. I used to
have no use for Chaucer. I had no use for God. It was easy
to settle for less than what I had put off wanting.
Someone to watch over me. It could even be Chaucer.
Hello, Geoffrey, got any good news?

Saturday
The coffee was good. This morning, my leg leapt up
as I stuck the needle in. Affirmation is not painless:
this needle is two inches long and it has to hit muscle.
My new voice has a depth I delight in but don't
know how to sing from. I tune my guitar up
and then back down, looking for a place
to place my new set of sounds.
Change changes. Changes change.
T may change me. I used to think the lyric was
but I can't change time. Is time so untraceable?
I've recorded my voice every week for a year.
I think I thought I could keep it this way. Small
museum of myself on my cell. I turn and face the strange.

Sunday
The coffee was good. The birds have so much to say this
      morning.
They whistle and chirp, calling to each other all over the yard.
It's nearly eighty here today; it's a relief; it's a reminder.
I want to ask the birds to tell me their take on climate change,
to know if they're scared, and how scared, so I know how
      scared to be.
How human, thinking alone in nonfinite clauses when I could
      just be
singing along to all of the good chitter-chatter.
I am habitually deferential. I'd like it if someone else could
      react first.

29

I know, embodiment doesn't happen as a statement,
but in a string of present participles.
We tease, but I'm not opposed to living, laughing, and loving.
What I can't imagine is laying an egg.
What could I know of what birds feel?

Monday*
I am sitting in the morning on the back step with my red dog.
I am sipping on my coffee as he sniffs what he has just smelled,
and he stands there, concentrating. I guess I can understand
    that:
I am still looking at the red dog when he looks up at me.

It is always good to see him; it is always good to be seen
by a someone who does love you, but respects their own primal
    needs.
I used to look the other way from the things I'd needed and
    wanted.
I'm trying to unlearn this, and instead I ask, what's wrong?

I almost didn't mention, but the coffee—it's always good.
See, I'm not scared to be different, I just want you to recognize
me each time we meet. On the outside of this poem
I can see myself, I'm watching, and so I turn my head.

To the you that's on the outside and ask, hey, can you see me?
No, I do not really see me cos I see my own reflection.
Then I want to say that I do til the words are only music
but while I'm waiting for an answer the dog has gotten hot.

Oh, these questions will persist I know a poem is not an answer,
but a church that we can live in.
It's a place to place my voice.
It's a still room still enough to hold the sound of all the change
    in it.

And I finish up my coffee and it's time to start the day.

I do-do-do-do-do-do, I do-do-do-do-do-do
I do-do-do-do-do-do, I do-do-do-do-do-do

*This section is to be sung to the tune of "Tom's Diner."

Temperance (Tick Field)

I live in the city my grandfather was an orphan in.
Rather, one of them. When I think about his child-body,
I always think about the loneliness all children feel
and his especially. When I think about my child-body,
my now-body moves through what it asked me not to
remember. I didn't. Then did. What happened happens,
unconcerned with time. Today I remember visiting him,
driven up from Florida to Georgia, my little six-year-old
hands, what they did, and how the gestures replicate in these
hands I have now: fingers running through down looking
for bumps through the sweat and the clay, pulling ticks
from my legs, from some half-wild dog belonging
to a neighbor. She lay in the dirt under my fingers parting
her fur. An uncle (who wasn't) told me to stand up
and back away real slowly. It hadn't occurred to me
to be scared of the dog in my lap. A girl back then,
I'd already seen how some men liked to kick, then hit
what bit back. I was afraid because I was a boy, and boys
become men, and I did not want to be a man. It's funny.
When I think back to my childhood, there is always a dog
in the frame, but that can't be true. I am thinking of
my granddaddy, on those very worst nights, his fingers
guiding my sleep-heavy hands across his body—no one there
but me to bark. My fingers found no ticks on him. There was
nothing to free. I'm glad he died years before he could hate me
man to man, me: a man who loves men, a man who loves
my life enough to figure out how to mourn whatever it was
he was seeking against my skin. This is what it means to
mourn the children we both had been, and to mourn
the difficult men we both became. It was never a dog's job
to save me. I am sure that dog that day was hungry.
I did not feed her; I was too afraid of the small troubles
I'd been taught to fear. But we did sit together for a while

keeping each other company that day, shedding a little of what ailed us so.

Temperance (Potager)

Riding my bike is a daily task that takes well to a little flavor.
When I ride my bike I become a mysterious and better version
    of myself.
I imagine myself timeless, placeless, crooned along by the
    soundtrack
I've curated specifically for my commute each day to make
it feel like I am the protagonist in a film that only has
about twenty minutes left. *How will I know if he really loves me?*
I look forward to finding out. Some of the people I love and
    respect
have told me that I am patient. I think I'm just curious,
and always seeking out a bit more, any reason really, for a little
    anticipation.
Maybe these are not irreconcilable interpretations. I am not too
interested in irreconcilable interpretations. I imagine the truth
    is always
more and less interesting. Like how when people pronounce
words beautifully, it's like *of course*, but sometimes a word
is spoken in such a disorienting way that it changes everything.
You can't unknow what's been revealed to you. *Chest levee,*
my father says. He does not know how to speak French. *C'est la
    vie,*
I don't either, but I do insist on calling my garden a *potager.*
The thing is: to have a *potager* you have to plant a *potager.*
Don't go looking for an allegory. I mean only and exactly that.
My bike blew its tire when I rode it over a discarded CO_2
    cartridge,
isn't that a big joke,
so now I listen to my biking playlist while doing anything
that could use a little flavor. Everything could use a little flavor.
Hence the *potager.* So I listen while I plant the seeds James
got me for free from the grocery store because they're from last
    year.

What is *last year* to a seed? To garden is innately to decide to
    wait,
or else, to wait to decide. To plan a decision you plant: a
    decision.
A seed. To plant is to cede control. Can't control the seed.
Can be the weather. A little water here and there.
A lamp, if you're fancy. Some sun if you're spontaneous.
I had an idea for a little *potager*. I had an idea for a little poem.
Temperance and I, temperance and me, we're on our way now.
I'll put it all in the dirt here. See what happens.

Blessed Are the Dead Who Die in Alabama

1. Morning breaks open: a jar of last summer's tomatoes shatters against a cupboard. Oscar leaves
2. For the making of it you need a couple miles, ten pounds of corn, & a jug of water in each son's hands.
3. There's a hate one has to have to drink heads: the boiling it does of the insides of you.
4. How do I explain what happened on that mountain? Sand Mountain isn't a mountain at all,
5. Grace, can you tell me about the night it ended? How you ran out & hid amongst the crops, belly

1. with a bang of the screen door. Off to find a bottle. Foreshots, heads—no mind, the work'll get
2. Brightest shine on Sand Mountain. Could smell it from heaven. Grace & Imogene sit up wondering
3. Grace knew it by the stink. Oscar would come home squealing, his tongue sliding down his throat
4. but a sandstone plateau: it was a sundown town that announced itself with a sign on the side & no one
5. down in the mud & him screaming across the yard? Did you pray, Grace? Did the clay pray back?

1. done. Rows of sugarcane crooked as a dog's leg & a half-foot too deep, worms coming forth like

36

2. who will come home & when. Oscar does them in, sets their
   teeth on edge. Grace prays, she asks
3. peeled raw by that poisoned song. There's a hate a man has
   to have in him to hit just to hurt.
4. can say for sure where else Oscar took his boys in the night.
   This is a white story.
5. I don't know how to know how you felt, or what you did
   next, but I've been told you can taste

---

1. a dozen baby's fingers. He tells his boys that you can tell the
   devil's in a split snake cos he'll
2. God for something terrible, kneels down to strike him dead.
   The least You can do is spare
3. Grace closes the door to the children's room, but she can't
   keep the house clean of what they
4. Theirs was a white poor, a white Alabama, a white woman &
   a white man, & their four white
5. the singing smell of a hymn lifted, how it soaks into the seed:
   what does blood do to dirt, what does

---

1. join back by morning. It's why you bury the halves in
   separate holes. Baptist caution. "Lord,"
2. my children. She splits a copperhead in half by the hogs.
   Her sons drop both halves in a bucket,
3. were born of & into, those four babies yanked into all of his
   hate, the buckshot & mess of it.
4. children & their white God, white violences, white
   kindnesses, white fears & white prayers for
5. fear do to what grows from it? I need to know what's running
   through the future, what has always

1. my Nana Imogene said, "He kept us on just like that, telling lies with a bottle in his hand."
2. hiding their question under the porch, but the Devil keeps the broken creature for his own.
3. They all take to sleeping with their hands balled up, looking just like him in the night.
4. & white hate of a world they thought owed them something for being God-fearing, hungry & white.
5. been mine to mourn. I want to know because I want someone to remember.

6.

I know now, the future has always been there: back when Grace
      was just fifteen she & Oscar
were already burying their first son in the earth of Sand
      Mountain, back when I was born
& you tucked Grace's name in the middle of mine like a good
      omen, a lifelong prayer.
I didn't even know Oscar's name until I asked. No one
      bothered to mention it. He died well
before redemption, as most men do. It's no surprise it took so
      long to tell anyone I was one.
Being a man meant being the worst things anyone ever taught
      me a person could be.

7.

The last time I saw Imogene she told me her oldest brother—
      whom she loved enough that I
took his name when I changed mine—had Oscar's given name:
      ███. There is the blood
& the blood always wants something back. Every one of God's
      creations has a sense of humor,
even a bloodline. I speak my name & the blood chuckles in me.

38

Every trans person has their own
relationship to history, just like anyone else. What I mean to
    say: there are things I traded for this life
(my drinking, my voice, my father), but when I realized I was a
    man it didn't make me not a daughter.

8.
Imogene, this is all to say: I need you to teach me what I need
    to know to let you die. Tell me again:
what all goes in that dressing? What kind of salt do you set on
    the belly of the dead, & how many
days should you give the soul before you bury the body? Blessed
    are the dead who die in the Lord,
but what about here in Alabama? Imogene, what did you
    imagine the future to be back there
on that mountain, in the fever of your childhood? Eighty years
    later, I dream of all we might still heal from.
I want you to know I've been listening. When I shed these other
    first names, Grace is the one I keep.

Scott-Patrick Mitchell

The Other ___

My throat is thick with him. When I say his
name, I pronounce it as if it were a white
string of hope, ectoplasmic. My lips are
bruised. From speech. From sucking in air.
From holding my breath. Once, he broke
me, towering between my thighs. This is a
lie: he broke me many times. A rapturous
revelation. So many little deaths. His blue-
eyed sky cackling with lightning as he
struck me, again and again, only to become
mountainous landslide, crushing me.
Seismic love. A tectonic rip. The tsunami
of his hips, drowning me. And in the after,
his laughter at the small sea bloom of my
jokes. Big hands to callous and reef around
my own. A kiss before he'd return home. To
his wife. When he died, he died alone. In a
carpark. Beside the sea. Exhaust connected
to an ouroboros hose. Car filling with fumes.
I was The Other Man. But in the aftermath,
I just became The Other. The water dries
up. Leaves me arid. The heat of this grief
makes for mirage: I see him everywhere I go.
My throat fills with sand as I try to devour
him. Even my tears have become steam.

a love letter to my former drag personas who taught me how to be fearless

i.

your body is a dreamscape... beard becomes drag, smoke and ash... you peel it off... burn juniper to cleanse and sain... milk thistle, soothe the grain... paint away evensong of face... contour... bake... incongruent flesh, origami body... hidden in your hide, polyvalence... un-Cremaster self... let ornaments rise... into heat, a body becomes a new body... how an apple can be swallowed... Eden an orchard before a mirror and you, without an axe... coat skin in silk and padding... here, a golden thread, coiling between ether and other and mortality: this is where poems come from... you paint new name on lips as apogee, an omen, then comb hair to lift toward heaven... there is a death drop waiting inside your limbs...

ii.

you have been practicing for months: to walk in high heels, bring new self closer to Goddess... in the club, love... air kisses and sweetie, darling... each night you appear, introduce yourself by using a different name... Augury; Selene; Phoebe... let yourself be camper... Lisa Nucar; Clare Vouyant; Miss Direction... no one is ever a fixed point... remember: this is for the sheer beauty of beauty, of expression... or the revelry of personal revelation, revolution... dance: handbag house and trance... in the bathroom, reapply blush... there, above basin, a you who is so happy to meet you, finally... that grin: as wide as eclipsing light... euphoria in seeing self's anthem in reflection, and knowing all the words... sing them...

The Conversion of a Mary

We make love in your bed and the sheets turn into bible pages.
You hail Mary: rosary a rope around your throat. You tell me
how, at the age of nine, your mother locked you in a dog run,
your face a lipstick mess. You, still wearing her Sunday dress.
Kennel comfort. Wood remembers bark of trees. After that, you
started hearing voices: The Apostles of Assistance. Blessed be.
How they appear as a Burning Bush. Commandments of smoke,
they teach you to hitch, bow, bend. Every morning, stained linen
and the Assumption of Mary. Where does your body go after
each little death? Some days you are a thousand acres of Dead
Sea, scrolled around me. A plate in plaster, purple bruise, your
laughter. Extinguished cigarette on leg. Stations of the Cross.
Our bed has tenants. The voices make a covenant from three
feet of insecurity. I coo to you to come down off that ledge.
Because what is grief if not a sob, a spiral, a season refusing to
shift: I see your curls in the Marri tree. Your parents send you off
to convert, confess sin. Pray the gay away through electroshock
and The Crucifixion. Leviticus, Romans, Jude: these verses are
curses upon our kin. You return home as moonlight in jasmine,
a koi pond simmering. Lilac blossom of skin: you find rest in the
boughs of a tree, refused fruit of Eden. Now, I open cemetery
at night as if biting into the forbidden. Kangaroos tattoo the
way. Here, heartbreak is halogen, a streetlight, the same colour
as your crown. Whenever the Marri's flowers slant my lawn,
I cleanse the house. Then I write as if threnody, break down.
In three days, you roll back into my skull. I cannot wash clean
your dirt, your divinity. With palms bloody, you reach for me
and say *Oh Holy Spirit, pull me into your body*. Years later, a Royal
Commission: you are named as one of the victims.

Wayne Johns

Runner-Up, 2024 Saints and Sinners Poetry Contest

Spell to Alter the Past

Like you, I'm most concerned with time,
     with all things lost, what will and what
won't be reimbursed, what's insured,
     uncovered, what will it cost to fix
the roof, the leak that gutters down
     the hall, which tree sheltered,
which was felled, who first ripped hope
     up by the roots, who transplanted,
who reset the little hand of the bone
     clock in the hall, who stunted our
blooms, blessed the sills, who knew enough
     to witch the well, who turned
the dirt, who sealed the wall, who slaughtered
     all those animals, who grafted skin
onto this house, what whispered words
     coaxed fire out, then blessed this broken
bottle tree, this spirit caught, this cone
     of disappearing smoke, this medicined
and midnight brute, without a face, without
     a host, what bruise of lust, this grave
for shame. Move quicker now; it's almost time—
     come summer, come blizzard, come white
hurricane, come winter buds and hummingbirds,
     unstring our thoughts with morning song,
outside this room outside of time, the barred
     owls call all morning long: *come home*
to who? come home to you. now

43

Virga

for Rodney Jack

It's snowing, according to the radar.

    Blue mass moving slowly over the South,
    like the whale that calls on a frequency

so high they thought at first it called only
to itself. The clouds look sodden. The air

    so dry the snow gets reabsorbed as it falls
    like an almost remembered dream. The medium

        mimicked your voice breaking through static—
        it felt like combing for stations, or picking a lock,

the voice never getting closer or clearer before
vanishing back into white noise. First recorded

decades ago, many have searched but no one's ever found
the whale. Only its call. There's this quiet just before,

    distinct stillness after snowfall, before anything
        ruins the scene. Some still write to ask how you

        left the world, or what became of all your
    boxed-up words. They make this faint hum

sometimes, late at night, the computer
glowing in an empty room, files opening

    alphabetically and rearranging.

Your brother wrote to me again last week.
I've ignored him for a year now. Turns out,

>he can't stand silence. Still loves the sound
>>his own voice makes. Also, the sound

>>of your voice undone, or thwarted, a cruelty
>not to be confused with indifference. You

must be haunting him relentlessly. Though we

can't see it from here, even that unnamed statue
>in the park looks up. Like that image of you—

>a child inside an unshaken globe—nose to glass,
>>watching for the first flakes, so you could write

>>about it while it fell. That far south it was almost
>a myth. And though you'd never seen it, you

>still believed, and waited. Now nothing
melts or accumulates, but you keep falling.

Hinge

Only what lessens suffering is
worth saying? Someone beloved
said that. Also, the world
is a terrible place that thrives
on the pornography of despair.

He said, Weigh what you left
unfinished against what you might
still do (or might've done) in order
to find some measure of your accounting.
Of course, the answer always hinges
on the last terrible

or wonderful thing you witnessed.
Last night, in the Green Mountains:
a cloud the size of a suitcase
passed beneath a street lamp,
seeming to follow along the power line.
The problem, the only wonder
was, he wasn't there to notice.

Max Stone

Dead Boy

What about the dead boy?
It was/is May.
May like swoosh-fresh,
like deliberate touch
of cold, like proximity,
like *goddamn bright out here.*
It's spring & he loved
fresh-cut grass
& unending days.
Sickly downbeat
Dead Boy, you never
smiled, just rolled your eyes,
& it's hurting me.
Little fighter, blood knuckles,
walls your only victim.
Prized possessions
left in your tiny wake:
Superman action figure,
soccer cleats, rubber band ball.
Come back,
sleep in my bed again
beneath the dolphin blanket.
Remember what she told you
early in the morning,
what comes next:
as a girl, this is what you get:
non-attachment
—skin. But I was a boy
making the bed. Not unlike

my brothers.
But not like them, either.
In the steepness of mountain,
you saw death.
In the future,
you didn't see yourself
at all—
just a gash
in the painting.
You liked Mondays
because you hated
being home.
You hated school
because you sat alone.
You hated everything.
Except soccer practice.
Do I feel different?
We're chirping headlong
into the ceaseless, but first:
a celebration.
Hey, you, party boy,
sad boy,
out in the cosmos,
come back.
You've seen me
at my worst
& I know you're lookin' for a fix,
jonesing quick &—
It's time for you to become
a demon king,
like me.
Swaying, tingling,
in the purple light,
it'll be like
you were never
dead.

Blue-glass flames
tickling your skin.
I'll play your favorite song.
I'll take your picture
by the water.
Remnants of a party flung
across the room.
Another nighttime lifetime
last night.
Blurry eyes blur
the mirror,
but then I see
your face.
Your face
inside my face.
No need to be
angry anymore.
Remember
all the people
orbiting you
last night.
How they
love you.

Another Night Out in Reno

I am teeth-blue,
I feel baby-new.
Shivering on the beach
except I'm downtown,
shirt torn,
snagged by evil, errant,
bitch-ass branch.
White pants already ripped,
blood dripping
from my knee,
pooling in my shoe heel.
Secretly, I like being a mess.
Callous, skip-tripping
through town Thursday
night to Sunday morning.
Swim splash thrash.
You didn't see me last night.
No one did.
I have a twin—
Evil-I.
Thin skin, loose lips.
Forget what I said:
that was
my other brain.
It's like I've never
done this before,
but here I am again.
I keep going out
just to see if anything
will happen.
Does but doesn't.
At some point
I'll realize:

the nights all blur-fade:
one in the same.
Pressed pill.
Dizzy lights.
Awake all night.
Stars getting dizzy, too.
Burning out,
I'm drying up.
Let's just go home.

James Penha

As If a Werewolf

Puberty in an instant of recollection:
extrusion of bones, tendons, muscles
everywhere at once—toes and fingers,
shins and forearms, joints and skull—
hatches a grimace, precipitates a scream
heard on the moon; follicles bleed beard
and hair surrounding the most sensitive
of organs growing fatter, growing longer,
its sack of spheres expanding at a rate
$dV/dt=4\pi r^2 dr/dt$ with wild ejaculations,
cascade of saliva, seizure of desire,
incalculable, uncontrollable obsession;
and when the night is done the need
to ask a gypsy why a man like me must
have a man to bear, to hold, to love.

When Claude Rains It Pours

It won't be like *Abbott and Costello Meets Frankenstein*
or *King Kong*, movies that terrified me for weeks, I told
my mother. It's *The Invisible Man*. There's nothing to see.
Then why bother? she should have said, but gave in, and
we were both right really.
                          But to become an invisible man
is scary. To be looked at without being seen, to feel I am
not here. Where I am. With you. My heart, my soul, my eyes.

Graphology

The wrench from printing to cursive in primary school
wasn't the invitation to run. What eight year old prefers
sitting with blocks to racing down hallways? So let me
course. But need I stay between those lines? Must each
downward stroke parallel every other? Yes, to get full
marks, reproduce the alphabet above the blackboards,
and so I scripted like a nun! Like a sissy, said my brother.
Like a girl. Ironic, since I was a sissy hiding in perfection.
But I did free my pencils, liberate my ballpoint pens, as
everyone does sooner or later, never eschewing neatness,
perhaps, but allowing my letters like my attraction to boys
to scamper cattywampus in flowing strokes across fields
and faces and fonts, hearts and minds, limits and years
and pages of poems like this.

Transfer-mation

I had no desire for the temporary tattoos
sold on the Bali beach, but he—dark, well-
designed and artistic—and I laughed a whet
about where a gecko, an eagle, or a cobra
might decorate my body, and soon he took
me to a cheap motel room with once-white
walls beclouded now by amorphous tawny
silhouettes come from old seminal emissions.
On the walls? I wondered why till he set me
abed on my knees and fucked with such awful
abandon that my own shot caromed far enough
to bind with the fresco. Later, he gently applied
Michelangelo's hands detailed from the Creation
of Adam to my belly. They faded soon thereafter.

Nayelly Barrios

Triptych as Sacrament of Confession

*"and this water symbolizes baptism that now saves you also—not
the removal of dirt from the body but the pledge of a clear conscience
toward God." (1 Peter 3:21)*

1.
A wave, salt-heavy, slapped my face—
                          pulled me under.

When I was ten we went to the Gulf of Mexico. We all held
    hands. Started jumping waves.

Distracted by some message in the sky, I missed my cue to
    jump.

The sting in my eyes as my arms stretched toward a ray of
    light.

My mother's arm pulled me by the arm. Salt water spilled from
    my mouth.

2.
we file into Mass
        dip   our fingers

into a little golden bowl at the entrance

cool   wet   holy

        In the name

of the Father

of the Son

and of the Holy

Spirit

Amen.

3.
I dip my fingers into you
      a body of water

I have always
been afraid to navigate
Water that has always called to me
Water I wade in
Water I thrash in

Baptismal waters

We stop for a break   hydrate

Catch our breath   talk

you say you can not tell me how many women you have slept
    with
           a litany
     a litany
your name over and over and over and over

Triptych for Thirst

*"Jesus answered, 'Everyone who drinks this water
will be thirsty again.'"* (John 4:13)

1.
They always touch her feet after prayer, but her power lies in her crown
But that was out of my mother and my reach. I imagine taking
her head and laying it gently on my chest. Praying she will leave
her sorrows with me.

La Virgen's gaze settled on us each time. The glow of her sacred
green robe draped around her head. Our pleas, the live embers
of her glow.

We all returned to La Virgen day upon day. Thirsty for her
     mercy.
One ask is never enough for one sin.

2.
After a trek to her favorite childhood hideout
among the hills of San Luis Potosi,
panting, I plopped down next to the opuntia.
My mother brought out a switchblade.

It wasn't the first time I ate a prickly pear,
but it is the time I crave most. The opuntia's limbs
sagged with the weight of its prickly pears. I ate
freely and greedily. The fruit soft and cool through
my fingers. Its purple juice streaming down my palm,
down my wrist, onto the dry earth beneath me.

3.
Past the landscape of your belly,
You lock eyes with me as I begin my prayer.

58

In a LILLES page on Facebook, someone said it tastes like
    olives.
I hate olives, so I am glad you taste like citrus and roses.

My tongue runs through a litany of saints. None of them
    thirsty.
I recite my favorite bible verses,
especially the one about the rock and the water.
Did you know that saints are never thirsty?

From off in the distance, your prayer.

Ezra Adamo

red hallway

i will be a tendon in the morning—
soft patch of summer 6pm light
on my bed, where i atone hands, half-
face, wrist underbelly

don't ask me to be anything tonight
except someone eating; blurred
face in oil paints, smell of earth
and fat and ground teeth

Absolute Zero

the notch on her dress
is an exalted bird,

shadowed canvas,
thick paint: apprehensive,

arms around arms,
waist;

elephant ears bathe
near her ankles,

sprouted through
slow-sun hardwood,

green, green,
willowed sepia

of the room,
safe.

needle felt

we cradle—raw,

                  morning: body
                  at my window,
                  sweet ribs or
                  vines, bare
                  tendons, slick and
                  still flinching—

red bones—drape

                  mint powder,
                  oil, pressed and
                  to my collarbone,

over a chair,

                  left neck fire,
                  drowned candle, like

sharp measuring tape—

                  wrist ring, thumb to
                  pinky, thimbled
                  shadow—to be
s   maller,
                  smaller,

tongue lulled metal—

                  until—

i want birds

        go downstairs—

on my shoulders

        read a blueberry's
        skin, lost seeds,
        flowered calyx
        dismissed—

and green

        go upstairs,

against my spine

        measure my thighs, waist,
        again,
        white noise wish—
        want to see an opossum
        on the porch and rain and
        chaos

Luis Lopez-Maldonado

Observing This Body

I sometimes can't really feel-feel my feet—
the tingling sensation like the white noise on an 80s TV.
I sometimes find little marble-sized balls
beneath my brown skin, I push on them, and they hurt.

Doctor says they aren't cancerous—they're just fat—
and if they grow and hurt—really hurt-hurt—
then she can remove them scars and all:
I roll my eyes quietly and smile, reassuring her
that yes, sir, whatever you say,

but my red relies on fear and my fear doesn't understand
why my tummy bloats even on cold days,
why my triglycerides are increasing without permission,
and why the mirrors are telling me I'm becoming
an amalgamation of both mi papa y mi mama.

You know, I sometimes I drag myself out of bed thinking
is all of this already starting to rot starting to decay itself
like bad poetry like a burnt tortilla? Porque I be feeling
like I'm eighty like my abuelita, smelling of Vaporu and Talco:
but then I remember, if Frida did not need her feet

then neither do I.

I Don't See Race: Bullshit, It's There

Yo, bro, this poem is all about the status quo, you know, how
white people make more dough, ain't never called hoes, because
this stolen land houses truths hidden under lynchings and riots,
painful realities that light-skinned privileged peeps are normal
are original are discoverers: reality check, bitch — you cannot
"discover" something that already exists, because as we continue
to peel this country's skin we are exposed to maggots and lice,
to lies and cries, and the sun will rise tomorrow, and the youth
will continue trokiando peliando trabajando so their kids can be
called normal, can be celebrated for their black brown yellow
red skin — cliché, yes, I know, but when poetry calls for action
calls for political fashion, I will always answer with 6-inch heels
and MAC lipstick, my pockets overflowing overspilling with
education punctuation reputation turbulation manipulation,
and yes, I can spell and yes, I can rhyme, and no, Karen, I am
not available to cut your grass, clean your house, babysit your kid
because this right here, this fabulous queer brown man comes
from kings and queens from people of the sun of the pyramids
of jaguars and jade and turquoise and mud — ain't nobody got
time for your whiteness, Karen, ain't nobody got time for your
200-year-old lies: so take this poem and slam slam it on Hobby
Lobby cheap art, on Whole Foods orchids, on your taco-Tuesday
happy hours, but remember we were here first, and we're still
here. I am still here. We are still here. And I see race. It's a thing.

In Seven Days, Dios Created the World

but who cares, am I right?
there's no room for magic
in a community of unholiness,
no room for modern-day slavery
(can't pay my rent can't pay my bill$
ain't got insurance right now)

seven days is 10,080 minutes
which is more than enough time
to get slapped across the face,
face down ass-up,
up-up down-down left-right left-right select-start
(stop playing so many video games!)

if God wanted a perfect world
they should have created two women instead,
no room for toxic masculinity
COVID immunity racist scrutiny,
am I right? Siete dias to create
the beginning of the end,
do not pass Go and collect $200,
because in times like today
is when I question everything I know:

where is God? Jesus? Jesus (in Spanish)?

I Borrowed This Line from an Elder: Yo No Soy de la Migra

for Las Cafeteras

Yo no soy de la Migra, no soy de las leyes blancas de las
    fronteras igualadas,
because my mom and abuelita crossed and stayed,
because las mariposas cannot be owned by la migra
by undereducated, white-washed eyes,
you know la migra asked me the other day, "American citizen?"
and pointed at my brown body, at my bent-wrist queer vessel of
    a brown body,
and I gasped, because I'll always gasp,
because yo no soy de la Migra,
and I answered yes with a lower-case why? Why?
Like why are you asking me that? Porque, are you playing God,
playing a power-bottom, playing to cops and robbers?
But I ain't no criminal, no robber, no American.
Yo soy I am, braided from ten thousand tongues
five-point star piñatas, burnt cajeta
la sangre de Azteca Mezoteca Discoteca, fuck, even Manteca,
but not from la migra, not from systemic racism,
because my glitter falls like fall, falls like rain like stars,
like how we need to fall in love with our … translanguaging.

Agnes Hanying Ong

Would David to Martians She

Tearing the orange apart at
    dawn, what a sick little bird
of a horizon to care for, every unsettling

    a lingering God breaking up. Hello? So
she dances, along
    to the full-, the full-

moon-mirrored throat of an Adam-tree
    to slit to lintel, with turnstiles, that
sheathe the damned, oh, in reverse

    cilice so seduced to put on
Dear American Dick, like
    an ancient slug curling, hurling another howling into the
  lawn

mower, as though her teeth can finally fathom how
    many of meanings, does it take, to change
a lightbulb, to deliver us from until

    tenderness can sink to mercy, until mercy is
itself, a revolution of tenderness
    at the turnstiles, now that water is even

much queerer than
    cruel. Like a deer or deal or, Dear
American Dick of, of a cork- screw, under a smattering of

clock. But unless! Unless she has come
from hell, to come to the desert
　　　of our pearly gates

ajar, this is the way, that she would
　　　like to valley in an undergarment of giggle, a wringing
of gut and, god feelings to wiggle, glisten

　　　she would to Martians, glisten, glisten where
we can love, like slope of fire
　　　to crane or burn, inward, as small-s

spirit, alcohol to follow: the evacuated
　　　carapace of what once wasn't, was an
era of a knight, knight capped

with tiny letters on it.

Seek Goodness Gracious in Everything

Comes the end of the spirit
or quiet. Those
bumblebees from
heaven
      hurricane down and your hand, unstable
every other kind of
mahogany sky, just like
carbonara of parents masturbating on a cliff
wall, the one, without a scratch
      of a girlfriend, unstable
too, or two, a glee
of a bleakness oblique as
oh, sashaying. Too retired
fishnets. They are
      hung well, like reversed
Lot's wives, each
hanging like well,
well, well, well! How else, if surely
there is vicarious
      atonement? No, not atonement, just
prayers in the sand
soaking up this innocence of waves
only a minim away, from minims
stringing, down-down down to: earth the full of
      grace. Say you see the
night! It is turned on by O
turbulence, winter
winglet, turning the other cheek of
window pane and, she was such
      a big heart, in a glass
jar on a nightstand. She was feeling
her car, cold, and it moved
too like jaguar, right

enough to be slipping into incubus queen
     like cake of curious soap
under a bed or bath
tub, but does it matter
which? Sartre! Said it was great
tub of a bath, ah! Under which
     soap would slipping be, would
seek goodness gracious in everything, thus centering
prayer goes like this: gay sex, gay sex, gay
sex.

Mass-Ejection Ejection

Love me hard and long for it's been
a turning since slivers
of bees, of crystals seen through
crack; how little
is a world, dorm, dome
or dom. It's been
puke of peonies since the last
decasyllabic line. Like linen I want to crawl
into tears or sweat on this glass
eye, which, on, one cannot be betting but leaning, the rain
smoothing jazz. Lately,
it has become very difficult
for the rain, oh, to be angry or, apart. Rain
needs anger Viagra, oh, to get to this right
      sigh of history, oh, yet the rain is too high
      a hyena, bobbing and bobbing rubbery

into the hollow-
pointing ballot, into the ancient
slug goring vision like a clog made of ticktock-
ticktocking, too, into
the wind whispering Adderall cut across
incantation on the cross. What's more naïve than verse
when everything is butter and bottom of divinity
of your dearly, sincerely, oh, unkindly currently believing
sun, never-never going home, while
it booms sore, oh! Solar
flares up cute kitchenette wall a rain
-rain rain mower.

thy O

Needless to say why her two
aunts, while
home-
  shoaling all, spend all, spend every second of their free
    children making pickled
  eggs, air

-brained daffodils and
rhododendra, just because,
just because, it is just—so could
  they name every egg o, or *o*,
    or o o'all home
  -shoaled shoaling innocents, as Saint

Thérèse did in
her o-, o-ol' cell o, also—because it is just so
she could, one day, turn into a house
  cat o' Lisieux. This is a
    villanelle, no? O
  opens her eyes, and stares

o right in the! In the, in the, right
in the stares at what's o
left o' o, in the o o' o-cheap
  whiskey o bottle. O, really, doesn't feel like
  drinking o
  drinking o' it but

o the godder o' it begs
o not to
waste cheap
  whiskey o the more because: *there's this*
    just so

many a thirsty child in the world

o' aura
today so do remember—to be
imbibing's o's
        privilege and, and—(of course there's the and,
                and)—and, as far as, as far as,
        as far as everything goes,

you must have a good
attitude! To privilege cheap
whiskey in a
                bottle calling-, yodeling, yodeling to *piss*
        cries pissing *Christ*. Nonsense! Cries a bottle calling out to
o
        and calling- out to *o*

from across O balcony, O
        nonsense
calling out
        to o, like o's Blessèd
        Sacrament o, woe—and be me o'
        course softly, *thus* it spake: Why did you o leave

o leave me alone? Un-
partaken, unadorned? Do you think, o ———
Thus it *spake*, that your liver's so
        special? To be—committing your spirit released
        from: un-
        indentured service, to me, thy O?

C.W. Emerson

Japan

I dream I am having a dream from which I slowly awaken. In the dream, I am in Japan. The air is crisp and clean, newly born. Pain, my constant companion, is absent, leaving me feeling strangely alone, without a body. I am a wisp of aromatic smoke, nothing more. Blue smoke rising in the thin mountain air.

My father is dying. I can hear him calling out to me from a far distance. His voice is tentative, plaintive, apologetic for his failings. His many failings. And I think, *I must be in Japan because my father sounds so far away.*

I love my father, but he does not love me. For this, I resent him deeply. To him, I was an unnecessary child; my very existence diverted focus from him, from his needs, which were primal and necessary.

But now, on his deathbed, I accord him the respect I have always withheld. I walk a fine line between *duty* and *truth*. The tension is electrifying. I think to myself:

> *This is what death must be like:*
> *inevitable, irresistible, yet utterly terrifying.*
> *Creation, in all its perfection, suddenly set ablaze.*

My father is dying. Yet there is no heaven for him to occupy. Only worlds within worlds, expanding out beyond time into deep space. I try to imagine what it's like to have had a body, then to relinquish it at death. To go from being a wisp of smoke to the enclosure of a body, once again, at rebirth.

How disconcerting it must be, like visiting Japan for the first time. Everything turning in on itself, everything upside down.

I am at the end of a long, disconnected dream where neither *death* nor *longing* are ever acknowledged. This has been my life, until now. I have always longed for my father's love. My longing extends out beyond the universe, outside the realm of time, transcends its initial object.

It is a plume of blue smoke rising high above Shimogamo Temple—*I am rising, a wisp of blue*—up and up, through the clean mountain air. To a place where dreams are blown into existence.

The False Gardener

Before you go,
let me tell you this one thing:

> *all last winter and into the spring,*
> *death felt very close to me.*

It's not something I speak of often,
not dinner conversation, cocktail talk—

there were so many variables at play:

missing you, the you I'd conjured,
the life I'd claimed as mine—

marriage gave me the *how to be*,
a reason to hurl myself into the world

while my heart tried
to strike a balance,
to open, cleave to the possible,

to change at the root,
attend to the garden,
left, for the most part, untended.

Through late summer and into the fall,
we rarely spoke. You barely noticed.

I woke early each morning,
went to the garden,

moved stealthily
among the stunted plants,

pulling up bindweed, gathering dandelion,
spiriting it away.

I finally left to find relief
        from the terrible wrath of winter,

turned the wattage up past a sensible burn,
acetylene-torched the blue-green ice
beneath my own two feet.

When my guard was well and truly down—

            please understand,   *I was dismembered*—

what had been in hibernation
came roaring back to life—

            a pathogen, a lethal spore
            on a surgeon's scalpel or breathing tube,
            unbidden.

The prospect of death
became real to me then,

            death by suffocation,

my demise no longer
some outlandish, distant notion,

our divorce just one component
of a much more Byzantine plan.

And so began
the time of my *pathology*,

78

of not being believed,
                or at best, misunderstood,
whilst you remained devoid
of any deep, caring function.

I was spellbound, paralyzed—
                that is, until today.

The garden remains, its care and feeding.
I'll gather the hose, the rake and hoe
                for watering, seeding,

the poison pellets to kill the weeds.

Before you go, let me ask you
                this one last thing:

you understand, don't you,
that we're not quite finished?

Expect me.

I promise:

                I will not be long coming.

Diva

She is alone on a stage, held in an arc of blue-tinged light from a single caged bulb atop a lamppost—the light is harsh and unforgiving. In the pixelated photographs I keep on my phone, we are similarly held, as if in amber, in a flash, in a spark of unnatural, manmade light, unmoving, unmoved, facsimiles of ourselves, the selves we once were or purported to be, nothing of earth or sky in our mien, no cirrus, no humus, no night-bloom of jasmine redolent in our hair.

We are reduced to pixels arranged on an incandescent screen, bereft of bone and sweat, no chemical cascade that leaves behind a lover's particular flavor, her unmistakable musk. Alone, orphaned, like the woman onstage preparing to sing, her intake of breath expanding her diaphragm, lifting her torso while pushing the small heft of her body down, grounded, held in the spotlight.

> In moments like these, I envision

a woman, one I know to be composed of flesh and blood, and no solid object—nothing broken or petrified, shocked into entropy—could ever pass through her, could ever produce that frequency—*listen, she is about to sing*—from the bone-against-bone of her beginning to the steady gain of strength from song to song—

the sweat on her temple, the clutch of her two hands on the microphone, and she becomes, once again, widowed, solitary, each note containing all the pathos of a full life, richly lived, an existence that was nothing she could have planned.

And now, as she steps into the golden limelight that envelops the stage, she is amorphous, formless, as light and lithe as a girl half her age—then, the doyenne lamenting her own lost youth, the transience of beauty—she is trying to tell us, *believe in me.*

I Lived for Art, I Lived for Love

As I approached the house, I could hear the soft click of your record player and the dark hum of a woman's voice, shaded in blue, emanating from your window. If I had to describe in detail the color, the hue of the voice, of the moon-shadow and the moon, I would say *indigo*.

I could hear the movement of the music as waves of sound refracted off the snowbanks around me, chords progressing from minor to major then back again, minor seven chords scaling upward to create tension that the voice would then resolve, bringing all back into order with the solidity of a major fourth, letting the ear rest for a moment, just long enough for the listener to identify the song—no, the aria—it was "Vissi D'Arte" from Puccini's opera *Tosca*.

*

There was no doubt as to the singer's identity, even without a closer, more nuanced listening, I knew who it was, who it had to be. You would be waiting for that penultimate phrase, the one you'd heard hundreds of times before, where the singer eschews the need for a breath—and all other singers require one—in the middle of the word "signore." Then, the voice takes two steps down, perfectly balanced, to end the phrase in the most exquisitely controlled pianissimo.

It could only be Caballé.

*

In the dream, as in our waking life, you were a creature of

extreme habit, easy to predict. Years earlier, I knew to expect your terse note when, post break-up, I tried to abscond with my favorite recording:

"The album of Puccini arias is not a gift to you. Please see that it is returned, posthaste." As Tosca discovered, "living for art, living for love" does not necessarily guarantee the best, most hoped-for result.

∗

In the dream once again, walking barefoot in the snow, walking backwards, entranced by the blueness of the air yet longing for the sun-risen promise of being there with you, warm, golden, in your room, in your arms. You were still alive. Caballé had yet to sing that last phrase. The air and sky had turned from cobalt to navy to a new shade of blue, just shy of a dark turquoise.

I could still breathe freely, could still hear that aria not as an indictment of God and of my own life, but as a work of art separate and apart from me, from the life I'd lived and would go on living. None of us would remain as we were, flung out of one dimension into another, but that is another dream entirely.

Daniel Meltz

Broken Monitor

I have always had this eagerness to go, to
leave the party or escape the restaurant or slip
away from the ceremony celebrating the
ancestral limestone monoliths in the fire circle.

When is this sacrament over already?
Please stop your jabbering, jesus.
You mean this movie's two hours and 47 minutes?
Get me out of here.

Even with you after that Saturday
of
deeper cahoots expressed
in
kisses the saints must kiss
and
orgasms (one with words one without) as thrilling
as the transubstantiation of a jalopy into a
Cadillac, I left as soon as I could because you had seen
so much of what I sought to hide desperately
so I desperately fled
toward the
relief of a flatter interior as cheerless as
an Olympic
butterfly swimmer who's disappointed that he won.

I have always had this eagerness to go and come back and
go forever and never come back but it was different after the
batteries died in both your clocks and my therapist told me that

the doldrums cover the smirks and the smirks conceal the hurt
so we mixed the colors smirkless and knew each other better,
adjusting our paces and relaxing our resistance and remembering
that the lame clichés of *Call Me by Your Name* were a reflection of
nothing!! yet

YOU made the difference my rough-cut
romantic who can't say anything about love
but can *do everything* about love
and I could lie around
forever on the sectional sofa

of your abiding openness and
defiant mispronouncings but
who are you anyway until now
I didn't know
convenient vision shimmering
until the removal was removed.

Variations on a Theme by Silver Convention

I was panning a lovesick video camera across West 57th Street,
    up that rise past the
bygone Playboy Theater and gothically sooty Carnegie Hall. I
    was busy immortalizing
wiglet meringues and patchwork jackets and salacious looks
    over Ari Onassis

sunglasses although the sky could not have been queasier, a
    sun-blocking butternut
tragedy color, as a garbage tornado sent a Milky Way wrapper
    and a *Daily News*
with a Mafia headline up toward the WALK/DON'T WALK
    contraption. I was walking

without a purpose, ad-libbing a percussion to the syncopated
    whisper of corduroy
pants and the wham of the air around the boulevard Blutos
    who steamrollered past
me and the jangle of a carriage horse's agitated gag snaffle. I
    managed my progress

with *no body* to contain me, just the whir of the Super 8 in my
    brain and the grace of
anonymity as I angled down Eighth, where *not one face* took a
    look at me, only
clouds pirouetting out of gutters and stovepipes as traffic played
    a rhythm on a

hundred-year-old manhole cover. Luckily I was tall already,
    even at age fourteen, so at least
I enjoyed the delusion of a presence. Though it wasn't until I
    moved in with Rick a
few years later—Rick X, who would become that public access

porno

phenomenon—cantankerous, absurdly macho, down-with-the-
    government
Ricky—that I learned I had an actual body (it had something
    to do with his filthy
imagination and his stubby Crayola fingers) but then I forgot I
    had a body when he

dumped me at the Gilded Grape (only five months together; I
    never wanted it to
end) because I'd failed to seduce a sailor for a Valentine's
    threesome. I remembered I
had a body again in April 1980 when I danced and stripped
    and sold the same body

for a couple of weekends and the week in between. (Not as
    dismal as it sounds.) But
I regressed to the mean of misery after that, when I
    reconnected with Florindo of
the scissored jaw and back acne who did everything he could to
    crush my body.

(What exactly was it that I wanted him to crush? Why was it so
    gratifying to kvetch
about him?) Then at the Boy Bar a few months later I picked
    up Pierre—no
accident—he was lean and happy (I determined it would only
    take Just. This.

Much. To change Absolutely. Everything)—and we made love
    all night, no sleep
whatsoever, full strangers he and I (he came twice; I came three
    times), a magical
glow that still radiates off those pages in my diary to this day. I
    exodused from that

lovenest, however, lickety-split, like Moses out of Egypt (just
    matzah and water for
me; I'm serious) until a couple days later, back on 57th, after
    Pierre had kept calling
me, after he actually tracked me down at work and asked me
    what was wrong with

me that I didn't want to see him again, "I mean I could
    understand if you were
incredibly *reesh* or incredibly handsome, but even *zen*," and like
    a moose in a
heatwave who never loses touch with its moose body I
    understood I was here in

New York, as here as the soot and the Solow building, and I
    knew where the insight
came from—from the literal hereness of my actual body—from
    Pierre's
participation in that actual body—and so I saw him again,
    maybe eleven times total,

because no, sadly, we never fell in love, but his challenge took
    root in me and became
my own portion and so to those who say There's Never Any
    Answer, There
Ain't No Answer, That's the Answer I say in all probability you
    gave up too soon.

The Old-Silver-Jewelry Smell of Oncoming Rain

It is one thing to be in love with you and
another thing to be in a waiting room with you
where I remember waiting in a cubicle with you
and re-understanding what love meant six years after
the last love,
you and your
overlay transparencies, sloshed by your
very presence and its memories of the weekend—a
terrible movie, a completely forgettable movie—
and the plates I broke in the dishwasher—
it was all a drunken accident—which you
later referred to as Kristallnacht

and the cedarwood fire
in the upstairs fireplace a couple hours later.
The sexy setups you whispered in my ear for almost
an hour, the noisy neighbors, the scandalous cats,
the counterpoint surprise of a
jealousy jangle the following
evening over family-style Peruvian (you never learned to
like it) because
Toby had not yet taken me seriously
and you waited in that cubicle among (as I started to say)
the overlays of you, the breaking teletype bulletins of you, of
a second you in your skintight Amazons,
in your midday malaise,
an hour and fifteen cantilevered minutes on the phone
with you, mesmerizing minutes, naturally measured
minutes, so unlike the minutes on the phone with
my sister.
The untreated wood grains and shellacs of this love
that keeps me reconquering with love

89

among the improvised prefab barracks
of me, as well as of you, the raggedy emotional flatness
of your living spread out on bedspreads
and armchairs and San Sebastian tabletops,
the delicate antique Carmen Mirandas
with the holes in their woven needlegrass head baskets,
the early kitchen boogaloos, the half-price tickets to
Trenton and Clifton and Boonton and Princeton,
the long walks under
hot walnuts (which look so much like hot trees of heaven)
(without the cigar smell)
though I'm sad to say
I would've left you without regret if
I were forty years younger
and gone to a bar right after, a
bar where no one knew me,
and drunk nine drinks until the thunderstorms
scuttled across into Connecticut.

A Poem About Everything

Mostly all I want is what I'm used to. Like his picture lighting
the dark when my cell phone yodels. (The sunglasses shot.
Sending hoodoo up my back.) And that moment when the
    message
PROBABLE SCAM shows up in the same blinding quadragon,
    a nightly
mystery sales pitch in Chinese. (Where in the world are they
    calling
from?) Life is change, yes, good, but minute by minute mostly it
isn't. It's the same six bazooka-proof friendships and their not
exactly platonic tingles, the same irritation of friendships of
obligation (two? two and a half?) and the familiar daily
    vanishing act
as I cede to the prerogative of whatever I'm reading, the
    funereal
monotony of the long lines at Capital One and the testing tents
    and
Trader Joe's, the elations of keychain library cards and stellar
    falafels
and easygoing orgasms and the truth sitting upright and
    shrieking
on a lunatic carousel of kangaroos and zebras. It's the pleasures
    of
pep pills and finally a quilting of measurable snow and the
    fingering
of elbow scabs and the knowing I'm right and the knowing
how long all along I've been wrong, how long is that, Steve?

But it's nothing like any of that, no, not really, not after a while,
because the posters keep changing and the Tylenol's working
    and
the epiphanies mount and the worries recede like the flood
at the foot of Noah's volcanoes. I have dropped to my knees at

the altar of false enthusiasm and stood at the crossroads where
the GPS had no idea, but I climbed in quietly to the backseat
of whichever town car stopped to pick me up and it was he
    who
was patient there, him in the back, predictor of every possible
plot twist, Señor Casanova-Gatsby-Hamlet, minus the nail
    polish,
minus the melodrama, tosser of wisecracks and bocce balls
    knocking
other bocce balls out of the way enough to say You weren't
    really
paying attention, amigo. There were people who were nice to
    you.

Hope Whynot

Nerves

The second first time we met
You held your hand out to mine and touched
Our palms together
Flat fingered to check the size
They were almost identical
Both with a slight tremor
That stilled once they touched
Our veins pathways that were always meant to overlap
But were severed that first first time we met
You tell me about that first first time as our hands grow busy
    again
Dropping vegetables we will only pretend to eat in the hot pot
    between us
Our bodies too full of nerves to make room for nourishment

The first being when you were fifteen
Hands shaking because you were too new to this earth
To know how to hold a thing too new to this earth
You named me Hope
Because hope was the last thing you had left to give

It's been seven years since the second first time we met
The nerves gave way to nourishment
And my life is full of you
But still the ache of missing you
When I'm six years old and have strep throat
Holding your hand to cross the street
You leading the way on our shared path
When you're buying groceries and I beg for the sugary cereal

The boring days
The little stuff

In those seven years you teach me how easy I am to love
You tell me that I have always been your hope

When I decide to get top surgery
We talk about the nerves they'll cut
The pieces of me they'll remove
I tell you how proud I am to be any bit of you
But that this bit just has to go
And so, you take care of me
After
I feel the nerves start to reconnect in disconcerting static
Reconnection is painful,
Even if it is your own flesh coming home to itself
I rest my head on your shoulder
You hold my hand
Fingers intertwined
Palms no longer pressed flatly together
Familiar
I listen to your heartbeat's reminder
"I am here, I am here, I am here"
And my own in refrain
"I am home"

Tell Me Where It Hurts

I tie you to the cross as you whisper the well-worn prayer made new in my ear: "For this is my body, which will be given up for you."

I transfer the blood tablets into your mouth with a kiss.

I take the book my mom sent to cure me off the altar and kneel before you with it open.

"Take this, all of you and drink from it, for this is the chalice of my blood, the blood of the new and eternal covenant, which will be poured out for you and for many for the forgiveness of sins."

If only my mother could see us make a mockery of her church as the blood from your mouth violates the pages that tell me how to "be a real woman" and "save myself." Would she finally, mercifully, lose hope?

This is not usually how your parties go. I don't usually have the power.

Normally, I watch you set your mark. The new blood you're trying to impress. You start with humor. Their jokes are the funniest you've ever heard. You grab their arm as you laugh. Make any excuse to touch them. Then, to get them alone, you read their tarot cards. You stare deeply into their eyes. Now that they are transfixed, you tell them about your trauma, throw in "how easy they are to talk to" to seal the deal. Then, you mysteriously retire to your bedroom together.

I've only seen your mask fall twice. Once, when you were at the tarot stage, I began to describe your ritual to your newest prospect. "Stop," you say, face flat, eyes devoid of their usual magic.

The second time was when you got rejected. It's rare for your ritual not to work. You find me sitting in an armchair and crawl into my lap, crying. I ask you to tell me where it hurts.

Later, once you are untied, I am the lucky one who makes it into your bedroom. I give you the simple pain you ask for. The one that knows its name and heals linearly. Just a flesh wound. Not the complicated pain our mothers gave us. Not the one that made our masks. I am all too happy to hurt you back. I am guilty even though you asked. How holy.

I take you into my mouth, suck instead of flick because I know how you like it. I am hungry to give, to atone.

Diana Burgos

La Llorona in Our Closets

       you are *La Llorona*
specter of a woman
dual citizen of the Americas
who always drowns
the memory of her children, her husband's last name,
under streams of Cabaret songs
wailed off-key

you are   *La Llorona*
whose body blossoms
in fragments
from the *sombras* in the closet—
the shadows
tucked between what remains
of *abuela's* sewing machine—
to conquer the edges of the bedroom
which keep you from the outside world

you do this because a mother
whispered the blueprints of your character
to an architect of the night—
to a girl named Lucerito,
who dreamt of
picking at the living room walls, of stealing
the silver her father hid
to smooth out the edges of the seven seas
with the bow of her own ship

you do this because the wedding dress you stole

from the last closet you lived in
is ripped and wet and stained
with *caimán* blood
from your lake dives and
            you're tired of pruned skin,
                    skirts that trip you,
                    keep you from running,
                    jam bits of you in branches—
                    into the hungry mouths of hotel dressers
                    beneath the footsteps of the folk
                    who chase you
                    to blame you
                            for teaching us how softness is lethal
                            each time you coil your long, black hair
                                    inside the throats of the
                                                    unfaithful,
                                    of the abusive,
                                    whose spouses you always
                                                    bewitch
                                        to snake them away
                                        from that pain
that's how we used to know you,
Llorona,
where we used to meet you
between the lullabies our parents would sing
to summon you, to have you pin us
in our sleep
and cry yourself across the growing length of us,
to drudge out all our wildness, our mischief,
            our delight from wanting
            those lips,
            those mouths,
            on *us*—
from our hearts,
through the soles of our feet,
purging us completely of the rot that is neighborhood

escandalo—
> remade docent,
> we sunk into our deaths,
> gasping into ourselves the fear
> of our becoming.

But for the first time since Hernán Cortés
> thrust his horses and church-funded destiny
> inside Tenochtitlán, inside its people
> and ripped your temples open to strip you
> of your name and face,
> you refuse

you refuse now

> to remain
>> *their Llorona*
> the one who pulses through major highways
> calling for us, asking where we went
> for generations, cursed
> to hurt the descendants of the same people
> you once vowed to protect—
> you remember yourself, Aztec goddess:

Cihuacōātl
Cihuacōātl
Cihuacōātl
> *You* remember how well *You* speak
> Nahuatl and Quechua and Chibcha
> and all the languages of all *Your* fragmented people
> how *You* wailed for them to remember themselves
> and still wail for them to join *You*
> in fighting to exist
> how they carried *You*
> into witness protection and seeded
> *You* inside the long robes of another

Mother Mary

Virgin Mary
Virgen María
>   who is forced now to tuck away *Your* many breasts
>   and snakes
>   and all our hunger
>   and can no longer birth
>   and father us, or any like us, ever again—
>   nor speak unless sanctioned to
>   by ***their*** stained-glass sketch of *Him*
>   who ***they*** gave unlimited power to create everything
>   but sex and love
>   between the ones they call
>   *those people*

For the first time since *You* ruled our old kingdoms,
since *You* lightened your skin
and crafted healing potions from *Your* tears while *You* lived in
>   ***their*** houses,
You can harmonize new songs
or train warriors again
or taste multiple lovers
or be *Your* own gender again
or pick *Your* own name for once
or join an improv team—
>   *You* are free
>   and *You* can choose to laugh too,
>   if *You* want,
>   to ripple the echoes of *Your* joy
>   across our bones
>   so they can rattle at us
>>   *Your* true story
>>   of how *You* came to remember who *You* loved,
>>   where *You* walk now—
>   how to shift and swivel inside us;
>   how they wish to speak *Us* into the world.

The Akateko

Rumor has it,
se dice por ahí
que este—that this
Akateko is a red human hand
hooked onto the limbs of a tree by a Japanese demon,
who uses it to fish us out of our office cubicles
before the wonder nesting in our soul dries out
under the AC vents

Rumor has it,
se dice por ahí
que este—that
Akateko—*ese Acateco*—
is a Mayan language thriving amid the juts, the clicks,
the contours of our pharynx

Your *Akateko* is the hand of a girl you'd long forgotten
who loved to wallpaper her mother's house with red handprints
and fatten them up with broad crayon strokes
so they'd become turkeys on Thanksgivings
and be reborn again as phoenixes
from the creases of bilingual "Get Well" cards

Your *Akateko* is your teenage lover's hand
swimming through the darkness of your twin bed sheets,
raw from its battles with your love handles, failed conquests
of your hips and the rest of your mother's heirlooms

Rumor has it
that Your *Akateko*
            files its nails
            against the bark of the your grandfather's tree,
            in front of the schoolyard, the days your cousin works

101

                                        hard to loosen
          his heavy Spanish accent
          when it earworms into his friends throughout games of
                                        tag and that
it slaps your hands with your mother's wooden spoon
each time you forget her ratio of water to rice,
or where to add accent marks and capitalize
so we don't call our father (*papá*)
the pope (*el Papa*)
or salt and eat him whole
as we would
a potato—*a papa*

Ben Kline

Runner-Up, 2024 Saints and Sinners Poetry Contest

"What is it tends you?"

> *after Michael Todd Cohen's letter from August 4, 2023*

Dad's random calls glue me to the wall on days

yellowed by Canadian fires the June I'm framed

gray above the smart thermostat set to 78, prompting

the shotput-shaped machine:

> Create a still life holographic visage, in the style of David
> Hockney with WWE muscularity, of a middle-aged man
> vexed by several consecutive deaths he may or may not
> believe are the cause of bad hearts, old grief and too
> much time

upon them, I'm grateful the peace lily has bloomed since
Dad said no flowers and the living mostly acquiesced. The
    wreaths

my sister-in-law's cousins sent had good hearts, new grief
I apply with neat bourbons, hot glue, strokes of lonely
    congealing

on my fingers: "Why does it keep rendering you without a
    mouth?"
                    EventhemachineknowsIfeeldifferentlythanI

say I want to feel the sadness
I felt for uncles too young
to look so decayed in their caskets

but I talk to this sad plastic kettlebell,
pushing up until the sweat looks earned.
Dad says he keeps busy looking

for ways to stay busy, to ignore time
doing what time does: gray hair,
the lily's white hood curling

into a brown coffin after the pollen
salts the pot soil. I tend to believe
I'm the soil, depending as much

as I do on water and sunlight,
the machine dappling my surfaces
with sparkle it imagines is the sun,

not a forearm descending:

> Recreate this image and remove the clothes from the
> central figure underwater and replace the overhead light
> with the shadow of The Rock about to cannonball into
> the pool, onto unknowing me, my mouth open wide.

Eventhemachineseeksfunintimesofsorrowl

say I want to art, but shit, I'm just ars poetica

from the Livejournal era, archived in vectors

between 00842 and 24800 until it makes sense

or the machine spits out a citation I can verify

is mine: "Why do you keep giving yourself over to it?"
                    EventhemachineunderstandstheonlytimeI

have I have to use now
now that I know
it's all now or it's nothing
that Mom started dying
halfway through her 5k
and my 10k after work
ends with a question: "Is red wine good for you after a run?"

> Studies show resveratrol can aid in recovery, providing anti-inflammatory relief even if more than one glass thwarts hydration and ruins dreams in which your mother will ask what you're doing here, again,

> making it all about you again.

I was supposed to be

a priest, until
I learned the plate
wasn't mine
to keep. God,
it seemed, had
jokes, tested them
on cocks I abutted
at The Dock,
The Pipeline and
Simon Says, where
I learned playing
pool in coral
flip flops meant
you never pay
for your shots.
I was supposed to
write comic books,
finish my novel
about gays between
crisis eras, be a good
boyfriend. I found
myself single, a door-
to-door agent to
change the city's
housing ordinance;
a chaos actor on
several sites, sending
back the same headless
torsos the priest
sent me.

Science and culture advance one gay wedding at a time

all the sex, matter and energy remaining
too much, an endless Red Rover
of lovers I can't name

racing for more space
and my time. I always go back
to lovers, don't I, several hundred

one-offs and a dozen boyfriends in rows
categorized by columns like *Scent* or *New
and/or Unusual Fetishes*, and then I blame them

for taking my energy, every matter too much,
trying to experience my every open end
like a quantum event,

innumerate possible outcomes,
but I only get invitations
to midweek three ways, weeklong

ceremonies on the Amalfi coast
instead of the thrill of anonymity
I wished lasted longer. Of course, I'm not

dismissing progress. Marry at will, queers. I'm here
for new forms of fucking, gay retirement
on Saturn, graphene space speedos,

free young minds undoing traditions
and norms, multiplying former binaries
like canaries in the gape, while I'm in the feckless grip

107

of waiting for new lovers to touch
who touch me back.
Send them over.

They can attend my wedding. They can tux.
Dance shirtless at the reception.
They can expend energy

on fake names, but I know
the formulae for lightspeed
scrolling my spreadsheet's empty cells,

the lovers who lied, who fleeted
by like diamine ghouls, their last
column labeled *Maybe / Maybe Not.*

Maybe

Maybe "Born This Way" is the new *We're here, we're queer.*
Maybe everyone is getting used to it.
Maybe bartenders spin like tin roosters on a roof.
Maybe cooking dinner at home is happiness. Maybe happiness
    is the wrong word.
Maybe describes our triad, our new house, Tom's pronouns,
    Bo's lost job.
Maybe we're too used to each other, too oak to bend.
Maybe getting used to it is a numbers game.
Maybe I've not licked enough butts. Maybe I've left good dicks
    untouched.
Maybe I've not trolled enough preachers who *protest too much.*
Maybe queer requires more of me than baring my stomata to
    thunder.
Maybe I like our new house, its half-acre yard, messy
    magnolias, and tiki lanterns.
Maybe not. Maybe I just don't know yet.
Maybe being here is my best offer.
Maybe I'll get used to it.

Raven Hinojosa

La Furiosa

I'm furious
La Furiosa
I could tear out chunks of hair
And light them on fire

I'm steaming, spitting, shitting mad
I could derail a train
And not get out of the way

I could claw my own face off
And kill a coyote
By shaking it in my skeleton teeth

I'm a bad wind
Hissed through the jaw of a terrible god
I twist off treetops and drop them on houses
Power lines are dental floss to me

I might dig a ravine with my anger
Take a torrential piss
And cackle rolling thunder
When the ravine becomes a canyon
And cleaves the country right down to the breast bone

And when Pacha Mama laughs
And rises to meet me
Heaving tidal waves, tornadoes, and bomb cyclones
With her swelling breasts and stomach

When she bares her perfect pointed teeth
Thrusting earthquakes that turn solids to liquids
And captures me in her massive thighs

Then I'll exhale
And sit my ass down
I'll take the beating, docile as a lamb
And wait for you to come home

Let God Do the Fucking

The air in here is listening, attentive
Leaning in to our love

We no longer move energy
But fall into the still center together

This rare space can be expansive or secluded
It can be inside or outside of time

We cast on and cast off genders
One after the other
Or, like tonight,
Forget that such a thing even exists

And just hold on
In the eternal, unbounded, numinous now
And let God do the fucking

We Share This Home

Who are you in intimate relationship with
Who gets to be a who
To you

Who of us was trapped in a lifeless diorama
Especially in the Covid years
And who was surrounded by friends

Of every quantity of legs
And whether they were inhaling or exhaling oxygen
And living together in the world

For me, it happened just in time
I knew about soulful consciousness
I knew it when I was knee high to a June bug

I knew that we were all
Made of some thing
Something lucid and cirrus and responsive

That when I knocked on the table
The table knocked back
A reflexive togetherness formed of tension
Like pulling a fabric at two corners

And that we two had a knowing
An inside joke
I knew that it knew that I knew
That there was no such thing as a solid

And yet I never could see
The heart in all those souls

I never knew to say hello and how do you do
And can I sit with you awhile

It took being taken into a native house
Taken in by trickery, as it turned out
But it was still the house that still lived
In the living world

I suppose that's why
I followed the breadcrumbs to begin with
To be among the speaking things
like Tree, and Bed, and Spider

Proper nouns
I took with me
When I ran away from that place

Now I live with Color
I live with Water, Stone
Lemon Tree and Lemon

They are my lovers and my siblings
And we share this home
A place made of wood and slate
Nothing slick or sticky that will melt when it rains

My favorite thing is to climb onto the bed
And array my books around me
Like a spread of cards

Ideas, language, memory
And spacious nothings
Settle together onto the coverlet
And turn to me with dark shining eyes

And hum

And I hum back
And together we find ourselves
Inside a song

I'm neither too skinny nor too fat now
My shape is my own
Not more or less

Even though my arm has a pair of ghastly ovals on it
A white moth worth of pinch marks
A place where the blood retreated under pressure

Even though there is injury that
My own heart's blood won't irrigate
It doesn't matter

The heart I couldn't hear
Now thrums all around me
It vibrates each of us

Named and unnamed
And our hearts thump back
Out of the principle of resonance

This is what time is
The sensed experience of
The great ticker's vascular rounds
Of generation and degeneration

Living as we do on a living thing
Table and I
Take a good bouncing
We beat in time

And sit together in a room full of other
Ancient quiet things, chanting

Light as a feather
Stiff as a board
In time to the biorhythm that animates us

You Are One Delicious Thing

You are one delicious thing

I press your towel to my face
Cedar needles, beeswax, notes of amber
And the essence of you

The same essence I see flashing in your eyes
Whether they are green or blue
And especially when they are blue

The same essence folded into flesh
The one that's made the mold of you
That, gender warrior that you are,
You took up the chisel of
And followed into the marble

You are goddamned delicious

I'm especially delirious for your pauses
The placid lakes between words
And the sweet dark worlds that flourish there

I like to think that when the world hears
These Erato-soaked sheets
Their eyes will turn to you
Where you are leaning against the bookcase
Hands in pockets

Their wondering will settle on your regular beauty
Your compact body
Your unwavering gaze

And everyone will get a taste

A tip of the tongue
A swirl of the glass
Because you absorb as you radiate

Their glances will find soft landing places
Received with leonine fatality
Just as my murmured adorations do

2024 Contributors

Ezra Adamo is a student from New Orleans. He was a runner-up in 2021 and a finalist in 2022 for the Saints and Sinners Poetry Competition.

A Rio Grande Valley borderlands native, **Nayelly Barrios** earned an MFA in Poetry from McNeese State University. An activist, she is a co-founder of Angry Tias and Abuelas of the Rio Grande Valley, an organization that advocates for immigrant rights and received the 2019 Robert F. Kennedy Human Rights Award. She loves to read, write, clean her house, sit on her porch, and spend time with her dogs. She's currently writing a YA novel about a young Mexican girl who steps into her sapphic truth—family, community, church, and even herself be damned. It is a what-coulda'-been-moir, and quite cathartic.

Diana Burgos was originally born in Bogotá, Colombia, moved to Florida when she was six, and has successfully cohabited with iguanas for almost three decades. She viciously sparred with the bilingual reimaginings of Colombian folktales and other mythological creatures for her MFA in fiction. She plans to grapple with them again in future poems, stories, translations, and within the oral retellings of nail-biting ghost stories so she can haunt the childhoods of future generations.

Acie Clark is a writer from Florida, Georgia, and Alabama. They're currently teaching as a visiting assistant professor in poetry at the University of Central Arkansas. Their work can be found or is forthcoming in *Poet Lore*, *American Short Fiction*, *Passages North*, and *The Massachusetts Review*.

C.W. Emerson's work has received numerous international

awards and honors, including *Poetry International*'s C.P. Cavafy Poetry Prize (2018) and co-winner of *Poetry International's* Summer Chapbook competition (2023). His poetry was shortlisted for both The Montreal International Poetry Prize (2020) and for the International Beverly Prize for Literature (2019). Emerson's work has appeared in journals, including *Harvard Review*, *Crab Orchard Review*, *december*, *Greensboro Review*, and others. He is the author of a chapbook, *Off Coldwater Canyon* (The Poetry Box, 2021); and his debut poetry collection, *Luminous Body, Glittering Ash*, is forthcoming in 2024 from Eyewear Publishing Ltd.

Nat Gove is a poet and writer who is currently trying to figure out what the dust jacket on their hybrid manuscript is going to say. They are published in *Noyo Review*, *Postscript Magazine*, *Bayou Review*, *Snapdragon's Anthology*, and a few others. They listen to traditional jazz in New Orleans with their artistic partner and little red bean pup.

Jeremy Graves is a bestselling author on Buddhist meditation and cognitive psychology (*The Mind Illuminated*, Simon & Schuster). His poems have appeared in numerous journals, including *Sundog Lit* and *Mom Egg Review*. He has received grants from the Community of Writers and the University of California, Berkeley. A doctoral student in clinical psychology, he resides in San Francisco.

Raven Hinojosa is a queer Latinx author, a witch, and a survivor of sexual abuse. These four elements of identity and experience are interwoven throughout her work. Queer love, animist spirituality, mixed Latinx heritage, and the navigation of trauma, together with the exploration of place, define her work. She lives in the unceded Ohlone territory of Alameda, California. Raven has published articles on spirituality and co-authored the biography, *Full Circle: A Quest for Transformation*, from ACTA Publications in 2021. She holds a BA in Religious Studies from Tulane University.

Wayne Johns' poems have appeared in *Best New Poets*, *Poetry Daily*, *Verse Daily*, and *Ploughshares*, among others. His first book, *Antipsalm*, received the editor's choice prize from Unicorn Press. He is also the author of *The Exclusion Zone* (Rane Arroyo Chapbook Prize from Seven Kitchens Press) and *An Invisible Veil Between Us* (Frank O'Hara Chapbook Award). A former Lambda Literary Fellow in fiction, he is working on a novel, *Where Your Children Are*, about a couple of queer artists who vandalize Confederate monuments and burn down the Margaret Mitchell house in Atlanta in 1993. Originally from Atlanta, he lives in Greensboro, NC, with his husband and two rescue dogs.

Ben Kline (he/him) lives in Cincinnati, Ohio. Author of the chapbooks *Sagittarius A** and *Dead Uncles*, as well as the forthcoming full-length collection *It Was Never Supposed to Be*, Ben is a storyteller and poet whose work has appeared in *Poet Lore*, *Copper Nickel*, *MAYDAY*, *Florida Review*, *Bellingham Review*, *DIAGRAM*, *Poetry*, and other publications.

Luis Lopez-Maldonado (he/him, they/them) is a Xicanx poet, playwright, dancer, choreographer, and educator. He/They have two forthcoming books titled *Gay Poetics of the Passion* (FlowerSong Press, 2024) and *Mexican Bird* (Querencia Press, 2024). His/Their work has been seen in *The American Poetry Review*, Foglifter, *Public Pool*, and *Latina Outsiders: Remaking Latina Identity*, among many others. They earned a Master of Arts degree in Dance from Florida State University, and a Master of Fine Arts degree in Creative Writing from the University of Notre Dame. He/They are currently adding glitter to the Land of Enchantment, working for the public education system as a high school bilingual educator and special education teacher.

Daniel Meltz's book of poems, *It Wasn't Easy to Reach You*, will be published by Trail to Table Press next year. In a pre-publishing blurb, David Sedaris is calling the book "funny, bold and moving." Dan's poems have been published in *American Poetry*

Review, *Best New Poets 2012*, *Plume*, *Salamander*, *Tusculum Review*, *upstreet*, and lots of other journals. He's been nominated for four Pushcart Prizes and was a finalist in competitions held by seven independent presses. A retired technical writer and teacher of the deaf, he has a BA in English from Columbia and lives in Manhattan.

Scott-Patrick Mitchell is a non-binary poet and the recipient of the 2022 Red Room Poetry Fellowship. Mitchell's debut poetry collection, *Clean*, was released in 2022 and explores meth addiction, recovery, and the power of embracing queer identity and community as a way to heal. Clean has been shortlisted for the 2023 Prime Minister's Literary Awards, Book of the Year in the 2023 Western Australian Premier's Book Awards, and the Victorian Premier's Literary Awards.

Agnes Hanying Ong is a poet, queer disabled pansexual transdirectional poetry extremist, policed coconspirator of textual violence, and, along with her bilocating doppelgänger, sign of the peace. She lives in the Rust Belt State of Hoosier. Her writings have been recognized by the Academy of American Poets; *Chautauqua*'s Janus Prize; *New Orleans Review*'s Micro Essay Contest; *Black Warrior Review*'s Flash Fiction Contest; Commonwealth Foundation in London, United Kingdom; and here at the Saints & Sinners LGBTQ+ Literary Festival's Poetry Contest, as well as elsewhere. Her writings have been published by *Chicago Review*, *The Minnesota Review*, *Black Warrior Review*, *South Central Review*, *poets.org*, *The Carolina Quarterly*, *Rattle*, et al.

Expat New Yorker **James Penha** (he/him) has lived for the past three decades in Indonesia. Nominated for Pushcart Prizes in fiction and poetry, his work is widely published in journals and collections including previous Saints & Sinners anthologies. His newest chapbook of poems, *American Daguerreotypes*, is available for Kindle. Penha edits *The New Verse News*, an online journal of current-events poetry.

Max Stone is a poet from Reno, Nevada. He played soccer at Queens College in New York City before returning to Reno to earn his MFA in poetry and BA in English with a minor in book arts from the University of Nevada, Reno. He has received fellowships from Community of Writers and Sundress Academy for the Arts. He is the author of two chapbooks: *The Bisexual Lighting Makes Everyone Beautiful* (Ghost City Press) and *Temporary Preparations* (Bottlecap Press). His work has appeared in *& Change, fifth wheel press, Bender Zine, Night Coffee Lit, The Meadow, Sundress Publications,* and elsewhere.

Hope Whynot frequently writes on queerness, gender, adoption, and grief. They hold an Ed.M. in Education from the Harvard Graduate School of Education with a concentration in Identity Power and Justice. They are from Boston, MA, and share their life with two lovely partners and a perfect little rescue dog.

Holly Zhou is a poet and mixed-media artist from the California desert. Their collaborative poetry and art zines have been showcased at the Bluestockings Comic Fest and at the San Francisco Zine Fest. They are probably thinking about rocks or capybaras.

About Our Judge

Chen Chen is the author of two books of poetry, *Your Emergency Contact Has Experienced an Emergency* (BOA Editions, 2022) and *When I Grow Up I Want to Be a List of Further Possibilities* (BOA Editions, 2017), which was longlisted for the National Book Award and won the Thom Gunn Award, among other honors. His work appears in many publications, including *Poetry* and three editions of *The Best American Poetry*. He has received two Pushcart Prizes and fellowships from Kundiman, the National Endowment for the Arts, and United States Artists. He was the 2018-2022 Jacob Ziskind Poet-in-Residence at Brandeis University and currently teaches for the low-residency MFA programs at New England College and Stonecoast. He lives with his partner, Jeff Gilbert, and their pug, Mr. Rupert Giles.

About Our Editors

Jan Edwards Hemming's poetry and essays have appeared or are forthcoming in *Electric Literature, LIT, The Ilanot Review, FruitSlice, Kind of a Hurricane Press, Mantis, eMerge Magazine, Fail Better, Gingerbread House Literary Magazine, Scalawag, The Mackinac, McSweeney's Internet Tendency, The Rio Grande Review, Los Angeles Review of Books* Blog, and *Black Fox Literary Magazine*; and her poems "Bird" and "Oven" were each nominated for a Pushcart Prize. She holds an MFA in Poetry from NYU and a BA in English from LSU, has been awarded residencies from Virginia Center for Creative Arts and Vermont Studio Center, and co-edited the Saints & Sinners Literary Festival 2023 Poetry Anthology. She lives and works in New Orleans.

Paul J. Willis has over 28 years of experience in nonprofit management. He earned a B.S. degree in Psychology and a M.S. degree in Communication. He started his administrative work in 1992 as the co-director of the Holos Foundation in Minneapolis. The Foundation operated an alternative high school program for at-risk youth. Willis has been the executive director of the Tennessee Williams & New Orleans Literary Festival since 2004. He is the founder of the Saints and Sinners Literary Festival (established in 2003). Willis received the Publishing Triangle Award for Leadership (2019). This nationally recognized award is for service to the LGBTQ+ literary community and was presented at The New School in New York City.

About Our Cover Artist

Jacob Mitchell, Born 1997 in Shreveport, Louisiana, is an American photographic artist currently residing in New Orleans. He has exhibited in Louisiana Contemporary at Ogden Museum of Southern Art in 2020, as well as the following years of 2021-'23. At the beginning of 2022 Jacob had work showcased at the 6th Biennial National Juried Exhibition at School of Design, Louisiana Tech. His work has gained recognition throughout social media platforms and online publications. Jacob's most recent achievements include creating a commissioned photo for The New Yorker, receiving second place in the conceptual category of the Minimalist Photography Awards, & being a part of "NO DEAD ARTISTS" exhibition at Ferrara Showman Gallery.

Saints + Sinners Literary Festival

The first Saints and Sinners Literary Festival took place in May of 2003. The event started as a new initiative designed as an innovative way to reach the community with information about HIV/AIDS. It was also formed to bring the LGBTQ+ community together to celebrate the literary arts. Litera- ture has long nurtured hope and inspiration, and has provided an avenue of understanding. A steady stream of LGBTQ+ novels, short stories, poems, plays, and non-fiction works has served to awaken lesbians, gay men, bi- sexuals, and transgendered persons to the existence of others like them; to trace the outlines of a shared culture; and to bring the outside world into the emotional passages of LGBTQ+ life.

After the Stonewall Riots in New York City, gay literature finally came "out of the closet." In time, noted authors such as Dorothy Allison, Michael Cunningham, and Mark Doty (all past Saints' participants) were receiv- ing mainstream award recognition for their works. But there are still few opportunities for media attention of gay-themed books, and decreasing publishing options. This Festival helps to ensure that written work from the LGBTQ+ community will continue to have an outlet, and that people will have access to books that will help dispel stereotypes, alleviate isolation, and provide resources for personal wellness.

The event has since evolved into a program of the Tennessee Williams & New Orleans Literary Festival made possible by our premier sponsor the John Burton Harter Foundation. The Saints and Sinners LGBTQ+ Literary Festival works to achieve the following goals:

1. to create an environment for productive networking to ensure in- creased knowledge and dissemination of LGBTQ+ literature;

2. to provide an atmosphere for discussion, brainstorming, and the emergence of new ideas;
3. to recognize and honor writers, editors, and publishers who broke new ground and made it possible for LGBTQ+ books to reach an audience; and
4. to provide a forum for authors, editors, and publishers to talk about their work for the benefit of emerging writers, and for the enjoyment of readers of LGBTQ+ literature.

Saints and Sinners is an annual celebration that takes place in the heart of the French Quarter of New Orleans each spring. The Festival includes writing workshops, readings, panel discussions, literary walking tours, and a variety of special events. We also aim to inspire the written word through our short fiction contest, and our annual Saints and Sinners Emerging Writer Award sponsored by Rob Byrnes. Each year we induct individuals to our Saints and Sinners Hall of Fame. The Hall of Fame is intended to recognize people for their dedication to LGBTQ+ literature. Selected members have shown their passion for our literary community through various avenues including writing, promotion, publishing, editing, teaching, bookselling, and volunteerism.

Past year's inductees into the Saints and Sinners Literary Hall of Fame include: Dorothy Allison, Carol Anshaw, Ann Bannon, Samiya Bashir, Lucy Jane Bledsoe, Maureen Brady, Jericho Brown, Rob Byrnes, Patrick Califia, Louis Flint Ceci, Bernard Cooper, Timothy Cummings, Jameson Currier, Brenda Currin, Mark Doty, Mark Drake, Jim Duggins, Elana Dykewomon, Amie M. Evans, Otis Fennell, Michael Thomas Ford, Katherine V. Forrest, Nancy Garden, Jewelle Gomez, Jim Grimsley, David Groff, Tara Hardy, Ellen Hart, Greg Herren, Kenneth Holditch, Andrew Holleran, Candice Huber, Fay Jacobs, G. Winston James, Saeed Jones, Raphael Kadushin, Michele Karlsberg, Judith Katz, Moises Kaufman, Irena Klepfisz, Joan Larkin, Susan Larson, Lee Lynch, Jeff Mann, William J. Mann, Marianne K. Martin, Paula Martinac, Stephen McCauley, Val McDermid,

Mark Merlis, Tim Miller, Rip & Marsha Naquin-Delain, Michael Nava, Achy Obejas, Felice Picano, Radclyffe, J.M. Redmann, Lance Ringel, David Rosen, Carol Rosenfeld, Steven Saylor, Carol Seajay, Martin Sherman, Kelly Smith, Jack Sullivan, Carsen Taite, Cecilia Tan, Noel Twilbeck, Jr., Patricia Nell Warren, Jess Wells, Don Weise, Edmund White, Paul J. Willis, and Emanuel Xavier.

For more information about the Saints and Sinners Archangel Membership Program, visit: www.sasfest.org. Be sure to sign up for our e-newsletter for updates for future programs. We hope you will join other writers and bibliophiles for a weekend of literary revelry not to be missed!

"Saints & Sinners is hands down one of the best places to go to revive a writer's spirit. Imagine a gathering in which you can lean into conversations with some of the best writers and editors and agents in the country, all of them speaking frankly and passionately about the books, stories and people they love and hate and want most to record in some indelible way. Imagine a community that tells you truthfully what is happening with writing and publishing in the world you most want to reach. Imagine the flirting, the arguing, the teasing and praising and exchanging of not just vital information, but the whole spirit of queer arts and creating. Then imagine it all taking place on the sultry streets of New Orleans' French Quarter. That's Saints & Sinners—the best wellspring of inspiration and enthusiasm you are going to find. Go there."

—**Dorothy Allison**, National Book Award finalist for *Bastard Out of Carolina*, and author of the critically acclaimed novel *Cavedweller*.

www.ingramcontent.com/pod-product-compliance
Lightning Source LLC
Chambersburg PA
CBHW021005090426
42738CB00007B/668